Edited by HENRI DANIEL-ROPS of the Académie Française

SACRED LANGUAGES

IS VOLUME
116
OF THE
Twentieth Century Encyclopedia of Catholicism
UNDER SECTION
XI
CATHOLICISM AND LITERATURE
IT IS ALSO THE
35TH
VOLUME IN ORDER OF PUBLICATION

SACRED LANGUAGES

By PAUL AUVRAY,
PIERRE POULAIN and
ALBERT BLAISE

Translated from the French by J. TESTER

HAWTHORN BOOKS · PUBLISHERS · New York

First Edition, February, 1960

NIHIL OBSTAT

Joannes M. T. Barton, S.T.D., L.S.S.

   Censor Deputatus

IMPRIMATUR

E. Morrogh Bernard

   Vicarius Generalis

Westmonasterii, die XVII NOVEMBRIS MCMLIX

CONTENTS

PART I
HEBREW AND ARAMAIC
by Paul Auvray

PART II

GREEK

By Pierre Poulain

PART I

HEBREW AND ARAMAIC

by Paul Auvray

INTRODUCTION

Nowadays, specialists apart, no one reads the Bible in the original text. As for the New Testament, how many young graduates, who have just spent three or four years construing Demosthenes and Sophocles, still do not know that the Gospels were written in Greek and, if they want to read them, have recourse to a translation. The question does not even arise for the Old Testament: simply to say that it is in Hebrew is to admit that it is incomprehensible, completely to give up any idea of studying it. For most ordinary people Hebrew shares with Chinese the doubtful privilege of being essentially a closed and inaccessible world.

Why this odd prejudice? Doubtless because of the paucity of real Hebraists. Doubtless also because of the odd way Hebrew texts are presented: a language written from right to left, books which begin at the back, queer letters none of which looks like one of our own, a complicated system of points and accents—this is more than enough to deter a reader who is not forewarned. And, as if to discourage any stirrings of curiosity, there is added to these peculiarities a completely strange grammatical jargon in which one speaks of "qameç ḥaṭuph" and "bᵉghadhkᵉphath" and "quiescent shᵉwa" in the earliest lessons, to go on to the mysteries of "Niph'al" and "Hithpa'el", and of "Lamedh-He verbs" and "apocopated forms".[1] It looks as though everything has been done to raise an impassable barrier around Hebrew, so as to leave to the Hebraists their immense prestige in their devastating isolation.

Yet let us be honest about it! All this is but dust in the eyes, little obstacles that a slight effort will remove. If Hebrew is rid

[1] In the pages that follow every effort has been made to avoid this repellent jargon; but some current or convenient grammatical terms have been indicated in the notes to avoid too great unfamiliarity for those already initiated or for those who may undertake to become so.

of all the useless lumber and presented methodically and clearly, it is seen to be relatively easy, incomparably easier than Greek or Latin, and so accessible to most of the clergy and many laymen.

Not that everyone, without discrimination, is asked to make the effort needed to become what is called "a distinguished Hebrew scholar", so as to be able to read with ease all the books of the Bible. Account must be taken of taste and aptitude, and of needs. But everyone can acquire a sufficient acquaintance to follow an exegetical discussion turning on some point in the Hebrew text, or to grasp, with the help of a translation, some of the features of the original.

It is our ambition in the pages that follow to offer a first contact with the world of Hebrew and Aramaic, to break down some of the more obstinate of the prejudices we have mentioned, and to show that it is easy to begin on a study of the languages of the Bible. If it also happens that a desire to learn Hebrew is awakened by them, that will give their author the greatest satisfaction.

CHAPTER I

THE SEMITIC LANGUAGES

"These were the descendants of Noe's children, Sem, Cham and Japheth, through the sons that were born to them after the flood" (Gen. 10. 1). From this text comes the name of *Semitic languages*, used for the first time by Schlözer in 1781, and commonly used by linguists today.

The term "Semitic" is applied to a group of languages having common characteristics easily seen even by a superficial observer: an analogous group in our own times is that of the Romance languages developed from Latin, that is, French, Italian, Spanish, Portuguese and Rumanian. To take a few concrete examples: "father" is *'âb* in Hebrew, *'ab* in Aramaic, *abu* in Accadian, *'ab* in Arabic; "gazelle" is *ṣebî* in Hebrew, *tabyâ'* in Aramaic, *ṣabîtu* in Accadian and *ẓaby* in Arabic; "two" is *sheⁿnayim* in Hebrew, *'ishna'in* in Arabic, *shinâ* in Accadian and *terêin* in Aramaic. But however interesting these similarities in vocabulary may be, the linguist is readier to dwell on grammatical structure—agreement in the way possession is expressed, or in the tense systems of verbs—which reveal incontestably the common origin of the different languages of a group.

Spread for the most part over the Near East during the second millennium B.C., the Semitic languages form a family generally divided—despite a few disputable details—into three groups:

1. *North-eastern group*: Accadian, subdivided into two dialects, Assyrian and Babylonian; written in cuneiform characters from the third millennium on.

2. *North-western group,* comprising:

Aramaic and Syriac,
Ugaritic (the language of the Ras Shamra tablets),
Phoenician and other small local dialects,
Canaanitic and Hebrew.

3. *Southern group*: northern Arabic (the language of the Koran); southern Arabic and Ethiopian.

But it would be wrong to present the Semitic languages as one closed and independent family. Increasingly today there is a tendency to group them with ancient Egyptian, ancient Libyan, Berber and certain other East African tongues, to form the Semito-Chamitic family, somewhat analogous to the Indo-European family, which includes languages as different as those of the Teutonic, Slavonic, Celtic, Aryan, Italic, etc., branches.

Hebrew is the language which the Israelites learned from the Canaanites when they came into contact with them, and it remained in use among them until after the Babylonian exile, when it was gradually replaced, as the language of everyday speech, by Aramaic. But it remained the literary language throughout the Middle Ages and is still so today. Naturally, in the course of so many centuries, Hebrew has evolved in some important respects. But we have only slight evidence of this evolution before the Christian era. A few scattered glosses on the tablets (Accadian) from Tel el Amarna, of the fourteenth century B.C., a Moabite stele of the ninth century, and some rare inscriptions or documents of the Israelites[1]—that is all we have to trace the first developments of the Hebrew language.

Hebrew as we know it, and as it is normally taught, is the Hebrew of the Bible, a relatively uniform language, as the medieval rabbinical manuscripts have handed it down to us. Any account of Hebrew as a whole must start from there, filling in details and noticing small variations by reference to ancient records and comparative linguistics.

There is no question of setting out here the history of Hebrew

[1] Cf. *infra*, pp. 47 *seq.*

grammar; mention of three great pioneers must suffice. They are, David Qimhi ("Radaq") (1160–1235), the first true grammarian among the Jews, the author of *Miklol* ("Perfection"), to which modern scholars owe a good part of their grammatical terminology; Johannes Reuchlin, the famous humanist, and author of *De rudimentis hebraicis* (1506), the first work of its kind written by a Christian; and Wilhelm Gesenius (1786–1842), the author of a *Hebräische Grammatik* and a *Thesaurus linguae hebraicae* which are the starting points of modern scientific study of the language.

CHAPTER II

THE HEBREW SCRIPT

The first difficulty of Hebrew, and the chief difficulty even, if we are to believe the ordinary student, lies in its script. It constitutes the first barrier, which prevents a number of beginners getting any further than the alphabet. Yet the system of writing Hebrew has a rare perfection. It is far superior to all the older systems of syllabic writing, and in its own way it achieves a preciseness and exactitude which most modern languages might envy.

THE HEBREW ALPHABET

Hebrew was, of course, like all ancient languages, primarily a spoken language that for a long time was not written down and for a long time again only used writing on a small scale. The alphabet came to the Hebrews from Phoenicia, towards the end of the second millennium. It had twenty-two letters, representing the twenty-two consonantal sounds in Hebrew. This archaic alphabet (sometimes called Phoenician) was replaced a little before the Christian era by another, with square letters, borrowed from Aramaic and still in use today.

The archaic alphabet has a special interest for us since its letters lie behind most of those of the Greek and Latin alphabets. A simple comparison will show up the likenesses and differences (particularly the difference of "direction", the Hebrew alphabet being turned towards the left, the Greek towards the right); and it will be seen that the gutturals *'ayin* and *ḥeth,* which had no equivalents in Greek, were used, like the weak letters *'aleph, he, waw* and *yodh,* as vowels.

Forms (1) Archaic	Square	Name	Usual transcription	Value
ɬ	א	'aleph	'	glottal stop
ʡ	ב	beth	b (bh)	b (v)
∧	ג	gimel	g (gh)	g (g)
△	ד	daleth	d (dh)	d (th in *the*)
ʡ	ה	he	h	h
Y	ו	waw	w	w
⊥	ז	zayin	z	z
ਖ	ח	ḥeth	ḥ	*ch* as in *loch*
⊗	ט	ṭeth	ṭ	t (velar)
⋧	י	yodh	y	y
⋎	ך כ	kaph	k (kh)	k (k)
ℓ	ל	lamedh	l	l
⋓	ם מ	mem	m	m
⋎	ן נ	nun	n	n
⋥	ס	ṣamekh	ṣ	s (hard)
O	ע	'ayin	'	(2)
⊋	ף פ	pe	p (ph)	p (f, ph)
ℎ	ץ צ	çadhe	ç	s (hissed)
φ	ק	qoph	q	k (palatal)
⊿	ר	resh	r	r (palatal)
W	שׂ שׁ	sin, shin	s, sh	s (hard), sh
×	ת	taw	t, (th)	t (*th* in *thin*)

(1) In the square alphabet some letters have two forms; that on the right represents the *final* form, used at the end of a word.

(2) '*Ayin* has two sounds, a weaker guttural sound often represented in Greek by a rough breathing, and a stronger sound something like the Parisian *r*; in modern pronunciation it is usually not distinguished from '*aleph*.

What is striking about this alphabet is its clarity, its preciseness and its simplicity.

Its *clarity*, for each letter has its own characteristics, especially in the archaic forms. Even when they are used more or less cursively, as happens in the ancient ostraca,[1] they are easily read. If there are difficulties for us, they are difficulties of

[1] On the ostraca, see pp. 48 *seq.*; they are the most ancient records of cursive script in Palestine; papyri, being much more fragile, have not survived.

2—S.L.

pronunciation not of decipherment: so for the gutturals *'aleph* and *'ayin*, and for the velar ṭ and palatal *qoph*.

Its *preciseness* is even more striking. In this system there is strictly one sign for each consonantal sound and one sound for each letter (the aspirated consonants being usually mispronounced as fricatives, as we habitually mispronounce Greek φ, χ and θ). There is nothing in Hebrew, therefore, like the extraordinary caprices of English spelling, in which one letter may have many values, as *s=ss* and *z* in the one word *misuse* (verb) and is silent in *island*, and one sound is represented by more than one sign, as *sh* is written *sh* in *fish*, *ssi* in *fission*, *ti* in *nation*, *ci* in *official* and *ch* in *charade*. In Hebrew, the alphabet really seems to have been made to measure for the language it was to be used for, and the language seems scarcely to have changed much since its adoption.[2]

But the most indisputable characteristic of the system is its *simplicity*; at the same time it is its most perplexing feature. This is because ancient Hebrew writing was only consonantal, the vowel sounds being unexpressed in the script. This seems most strange to a western reader. If we wrote only the consonants, what would be left of such a phrase as *the book has been a great pleasure to read*? Or how should we distinguish between *free action*, *fur auction* and *fair caution*? But this only shows clearly the difference between the two idioms. In Hebrew, and more generally in Semitic, the consonantal structure of the language is much more radically fixed than in our own tongue. Normally, every Hebrew root is composed of three consonants. It does sometimes happen that one of these consonants is wanting or has disappeared, but there always remain at least two root consonants to which prefixes and suffixes are added to mark grammatical functions. Verbal forms like the Latin *aio*, the Greek οἴει or the French *ai eu* are inconceivable therefore in Hebrew. In the regular conjugation of the verb we write

---

[2] This only appears true, of course, to a superficial glance. Actually, specialists speak of two original values of *ḥeth* and *'ayin*, for example, corresponding to the Arabic letters ḥ and ḫ in the one case, and ' and gh in the other. But these are very similar sounds which came to be confused.

qṭl (*qaṭal*), *he has killed*, *qṭlt* (*qaṭalta*), *you have killed* (sing.), *qṭltm* (*qᵉṭaltem*), *you have killed* (plur.), *yqṭl* (*yiqṭol*), *he will kill*. All the forms are easily recognized as coming from the root *qṭl* and as denoting different tenses or different persons. For an Israelite a phrase like *hmlk qṭl 'th-hz'b* is unhesitatingly read as *hammelek qaṭal 'eth-hazzᵉ'eb*, "the king has killed the wolf".

All the same, not every sentence is so simple, and the consonantal script left room sometimes for ambiguities which their contexts were insufficient to resolve. So, very early on, the habit grew of marking certain vowel sounds that were particularly important either because of their position (final vowels) or their nature (long vowels), by using four consonants more or less naturally suited for such use: the sound of *yodh* shades easily into that of the vowel *i* (*yes* pronounced slowly becomes *i-es*); *waw* easily gives *u* (*watt* pronounced slowly gives *oo-att*; and cf. Fr. *oui*, Lat. *uir*, etc.); and two scarcely sounded letters, *'aleph* and *he*, which in certain cases were not felt as consonants at all and served only to support the vowel that went with them.[3] So some confusion could be avoided: for *qaṭal*, "he has killed" *qṭl* was still written; but for the feminine *qaṭᵉla*, "she has killed", *qṭlh* was written, for *qoṭel*, "killing", *qwṭl*, for *qaṭul*, "killed", *qṭwl*, etc., a system which was extended as time passed. It is clearly used more frequently in Chronicles than in the corresponding chapters of Kings. There was even some abuse of the practice in certain schools of scribes, but this was not general. But the custom of writing in certain vowel sounds was always a haphazard business; the same word, *gadol*, "great", is found written, sometimes even in the one book, at times *gdwl* and at others *gdl*,[4] with no apparent reason.

Such was the method of writing normal in Israel while Hebrew was the spoken language of every day. It could be called a modified consonantal system: consonantal, since it used only the twenty-two consonants of the alphabet and no other sign,

---

[3] These four letters are called *weak letters* because they easily lose their consonantal value and become *quiescent* (that is, not sounded). When they are used as vowels they are called *matres lectionis* ("helpers of reading").

[4] Writing with the *matres lectionis* is "full", that without is "defective".

and modified, because some of these letters could be used in certain cases to signify vowel sounds. It certainly did not reproduce exactly the pronunciation of Hebrew, but none of our modern scripts, though they are obviously more complicated, has ever claimed perfect exactitude. Such as it was, it represented sufficiently well, for the experienced reader, the current pronunciation. In our own day it has been taken up again by the Israelis, without any important changes, to write modern Hebrew. They only use vowel points for particularly difficult words, for example for foreign proper names, or in books for children and the sacred books. In their everyday usage they content themselves, like the ancient Israelites, and like the Arabs also, with a consonantal script; a sufficient proof of the satisfactoriness of the system.

WRITING THE VOWELS

But the day came when Hebrew ceased to be spoken by the Jewish people. From that time, the consonantal script was insufficient to represent and suggest the correct pronunciation. To make the correct decipherment of the text of the Bible easier for the ordinary Jew, and especially to prevent there being too many "howlers" in the readings in the synagogues, some rabbis, whom for the sake of brevity we call the Massoretes, though the name does not properly belong to them, set themselves to complete the system of writing by marking in all the vowels.

But just as this was happening the sacred character of the Bible text was being stressed: a single, unique text had been chosen and "canonized", which from then on had to be copied and recopied without any kind of alteration. To have added a single letter would have been a sacrilege.

Because of this double need, to mark all the vowels and to preserve the sacred text, the system of vowel points was devised. Not a letter of the text was changed, but it was completed by points or lines placed in, under or over the existing letters. Many systems of this kind were used in various times and places. That which finally prevailed and was adopted in the printed Bibles was that used in the manuscripts written by the family of ben Asher in the ninth and tenth centuries A.D., now known as the Massoretic system. Its origins must, however, go much further back.

The number of sounds to be represented was theoretically five: three primitive sounds, a, i, u, and two derived from these, e (from a fusion of a and i) and o (from a and u); that is, putting the most open sound (a) in the middle and the closed sounds at the ends:

$$i \qquad e \qquad a \qquad o \qquad u$$

Now three of these vowels can be pronounced as open or closed: a (and we shall mark them, arbitrarily, as a and â), o (o and ô), and e (e and ê). So that we get a series of eight vowel sounds which then reduces to seven because closed a and open o come together and are confused:

$$i \qquad ê \qquad e \qquad a \qquad \begin{Bmatrix} o \\ â \end{Bmatrix} \qquad ô \qquad u$$

For these seven vowels seven different signs were devised which were joined to the preceding consonant:

for i	one point under the consonant[5];
for ê	two points beside each other under the consonant;
for e	three points in an inverted triangle;
for a	a short horizontal line;
for o = â	a sign like a small capital (sans-serif) T;
for ô	a point *above* and to the left of the consonant;
for u	three points in a slanting line under the consonant.

To these seven signs an eighth was added, two points one above the other, written under the consonant to signify mute e (the sound of the *e* in *the cat*).

But in Hebrew as in every language some vowels were capable of variation in length, and this also was signified. Three of the vowels, the more open, e, a and o, could be shortened almost to the vague sound of mute e (cf. the sounds of these vowels in

[5] See table below.

the unstressed first syllables of *believe, against, correct*), and so these were written as the sign of the normal vowel combined with that of mute e. For the long vowels the position was more difficult, for they had already been customarily signified in script by the consonants *'aleph, he, waw* and *yodh*. It was therefore settled that the appropriate vowel points should be used together with the consonant already being used; but for the long u, to simplify things, it was enough to write a *single* point *in* the *waw*. So we get the following table[6]:

Vowels	i	ê	e	a	â o	ô	u	e
long	ִ	ֵ	ֶ			וֹ	וּ	
medium	ִ	ֵ	ֶ	ַ	ָ	ֹ	ֻ	
short			ֱ	ֲ	ֳ			ְ

Two other important signs should be noted: a diacritical point over *sin, shin*, as shown in the table of the alphabet; and the strengthening point put inside consonants, which has the effect of prolonging or doubling them, and which is marked in transcription by doubling the consonant.[7]

Here as an example is the first sentence of the Bible (Gen. 1. 1) in Hebrew and transcribed:

בְּרֵאשִׁית בָּרָא אֱלֹהִים אֵח הַשָּׁמַיִם וְאֵת הָאָרֶץ

berê'shîth bârâ' 'elôhîm 'êth hashâmayim we' êth hâ'âreç

---

[6] Naturally these vowels had names; i is *hireq*, e is *seghol*, a is *pathah*, â is *qameç*, and so on. There is no need to burden the memory with these. The only one to learn is the name for mute e: it is called *shewa*, or *simple shewa* (to distinguish it from the shortened e, a, o, which are sometimes called *compound shewas*).

[7] This point is called *dagesh*, or *dagesh forte*, as opposed to *dagesh lene*, which we shall deal with later.

Such are the essentials of the system of Hebrew writing.[8] No doubt it owes to its late and artificial character its quality of being remarkably rational. Its only illogicality lies in its writing long vowels generally (but not always) as a combination of consonants and vowel points. But that is because the Massoretes inherited a consonantal text which they could use but not dare to alter. This small point aside, one has only to compare our modern script to see the advantage of the system. It might be said that it is complicated. Perhaps it is, but only because it is precise. What would English writing be like if we wanted to distinguish between the short, open o of *rock* and the long, closed o of *roll*? Or between the three pronunciations of s in *use* (noun), *use* (verb) and *usual*? Or the four pronunciations of c in *count, cinema, cello* and *victuals*? And are there not worse complications with our diphthongs (ee represented in writing by ee, ie, ei, ea, e, i and y), without mentioning combinations of vowels and consonants (er, ir, ur, re, our, all representing er). Surely Hebrew is an easy language!

OTHER SIGNS

Hebrew writing does, however, have other less happy characteristics, which complicate it without adding any appreciable advantages.

First, the Massoretes decided, more or less arbitrarily, that

[8] The text of our Bibles, then, is made up of two elements: an ancient, sacred and unchangeable element, the consonantal text; and a recent element, subject to variation, the vowels added by the rabbis. This is the explanation of the odd phenomenon of the Q^ere and the K^ethibh, which is so puzzling for beginners. The Q^ere is a marginal variant which is *read* (Q^ere = "read") instead of what is actually *written* (K^ethibh = "written") in the traditional text. What complicates matters is that the rabbinical scholars, who could not introduce the variant they preferred into the text, which was inviolable, made up for that by putting the vowels of the word they preferred with the consonants of the written text. This is the origin of several apparently monstrous words, the most frequent and the most famous being "Jehovah", the fusion of the consonants of the ancient reading YHWH (Yahweh) and the vowels of the more recent variant '^{a}donai, "Lord". "Yahweh" was written, '^{a}donai was read, and no one who knew what he was doing would have dreamed of reading "Jehovah".

every non-final consonant should be marked with a vowel sign. When there was no vowel sound to represent, they chose to furnish the consonant with the same sign that normally represented mute e, two points vertically under the letter. In other words the double point (*sh^ewa*) then had two values, sometimes mute e, sometimes the absence of a vowel.[9] A word like *yiqt^elu*, "they will kill", is written with two *sh^ewas*, one under the *qoph* which is not pronounced, and the other under the *ṭeth* which represents a mute e. It is something like our mute e which is sometimes pronounced (*wanted*) and sometimes not (*lacked*).[10] Although this ambiguity does not constitute a serious difficulty for the practised reader it does give considerable trouble to the beginner.

There is another more serious ambiguity: the double value of *dagesh*. At the late period when the Massoretes were introducing this precise notation, six consonants (*beth, gimel, daleth, kaph, pe* and *taw*)[11] had two pronunciations. When they were doubled, or when they were not immediately preceded by any vowel, they kept their original plosive pronunciation; but when they were not doubled and followed immediately on a vowel they were pronounced as spirants, some of them not known in English: b became bh, conventionally pronounced v; p became ph, pronounced f; d became dh, pronounced like *th* in *this*; t, th as in *thin*; and g and k became more guttural, like the *gamma* and *chi* of modern Greek, written gh and kh and not distinguished from g and k in conventional pronunciation. Since the Massoretes wished to be meticulously precise, they needed to mark this difference in pronunciation, and generally "pointed" these letters inside when they were plosives, and wrote a short horizontal line above them when they were spirants. Later, in the printed Bibles, the line was left out and only the point inside the letter was left. Unfortunately the same sign was already

[9] The first is called *vocal* or *moving sh^ewa*, the second *quiescent* or *silent*.

[10] To complete the analogy we should have to write an e between any two consecutive consonants: *Heberew*, etc. Cf. the *sh^ewa* that is heard in the Northern Irish pronunciation of film: *fil^em*.

[11] Called "b^eghadhk^ephath" letters, the name being a mnemonic including them all.

also used to mark the doubling of a consonant (p. 22), so that this point, *dagesh*, was now ambiguous, having two uses: to show that a letter was doubled, and to show that certain letters should be pronounced as plosives. A little practice makes it possible to distinguish them easily, but it is an additional difficulty for beginners.

The last difficulty is this: our printed Bibles are furnished, in addition to the vowel points we have described, with a complicated system of accents designed to indicate, for reading, or rather for the public chanting of the text, both the position of the accent in each word and the relations of the words to one another. It thus corresponds roughly to Greek accentuation in one respect and to our punctuation in another. But it is much more complicated than both put together, being made up of no less than twenty signs.[12] If it is sometimes useful, it must be admitted that it is often perplexing, and it could serve the same purposes if it were considerably simplified.

PRACTICAL CONCLUSIONS

Given what has been said about the history of the Hebrew script, in conclusion, the following requirements might be put forward:

1. That beginners should only be introduced to *what is essential*; that is, not only that the teacher should leave aside the mysteries of the accentuation of the Bible text (that is generally done), but also that he should deliberately ignore the double pronunciation of certain letters (the "beghadhkephath" letters) so that an internal point in these letters always means that they are to be pronounced as plosives. It is easy to explain these peculiarities after a few months' practice in Hebrew, but it is never necessary to insist on their application in normal pronunciation.

2. On the other hand, as for the qualified Hebraists (and so

[12] There are really two systems of accents, one being used in most books of the Bible, and the other, called the poetic system, used in the three books, Job, Proverbs and Psalms; the first has twenty-one signs, the latter twenty.

above all for teachers), they should get into the habit of using *non-vocalized* texts, and this not as a kind of exercise or unusual procedure, but for most of their work. They must, of course, take account of the Massoretic tradition, but it would be a pity if that were always to constitute a screen between them and the text.

In other words, progress in Hebrew is envisaged in three stages:

1. The *introductory* stage, using the consonantal text with only those elements of the rabbinical tradition that are *useful*.

2. The *normal* stage, using the *printed text of the Bible*; that is, all the elements of the rabbinical tradition so far as concerns the text proper.

3. The *higher* stage, marked by the return to the *purely consonantal text*; that is, the Bible as it was when it was gathered together and the text fixed in the synagogue (about the first century A.D.).

But such reforms will only be possible, or at least effective, if texts of these kinds are provided. When will the day come when an editor with some courage will provide for scholars *a non-vocalized Bible*,[13] and for young students *texts* (selected to begin with) *with simplified vocalization*, that is, unencumbered by (a) the rabbinical accentuation, (b) the unpronounced double point, quiescent *sheʷa* or (c) the internal point which simply marks the plosive pronunciation of a consonant, *dagesh lene*?

Even prepared for by such indispensable editorial work, such a reform in teaching Hebrew would certainly run into serious difficulties: there would first be the simple inertia of established routine and the mysterious attachment men have to what they themselves suffered from.[14] But also there would be the im-

---

[13] Such works are occasionally to be found on the secondhand market, such as the magnificent *Biblia hebraica* of P. Houbigant, 4 in-fᵒ, Paris, 1753. But they are rare and expensive.

[14] In this respect the reaction of the Hebrew scholar is rather like that of the ordinary Englishman faced with a proposal to simplify English spelling: how can he want the removal of difficulties he struggled with throughout his childhood, which he now thinks he has overcome?

pression that the solution proposed, so far as concerns beginners, is an unhappy compromise, since it uses a text neither wholly rabbinical nor wholly archaic. That is true, but it is only a stage: after a year's introduction, of course, the student would go on to use the standard text, so as to apply himself later, if need be, to the archaic, non-vocalized text.

CHAPTER III

HEBREW NOUNS

It was said just now that Hebrew is an easy language; here, briefly, is the proof.

Whoever has at any time studied the classical languages preserves a somewhat gloomy recollection of the five declensions in Latin, and the three in Greek, themselves very much subdivided. There is nothing like that in Hebrew.

The ancient Semitic languages doubtless had cases, and grammarians believe that traces can be seen in Hebrew of a nominative in *u*, a genitive in *i* and an accusative in *a*, not forgetting "mimation", which consists in adding *mem* to the ends of nouns without a complement. But these are only relics, and in fact a Hebrew noun, say *sûs*, "horse", has the same form whether it is the subject, the direct or indirect object or even the complement of a noun. Usually its function is marked, as in our analytic languages, by a preposition or a particle: *'eth* indicates (optionally) the direct object of a verb; the three simple prepositions *le*, *be* and *ke*, which are joined to the noun, signifying "to", "in" and "like" (*kesûs*, "like a horse"); the slightly more complicated prepositions *'el*, *'al*, *'im*, etc. ("unto", "on" and "with") denoting other relations.

The whole problem then is to form the feminine and the plural (there is no neuter, but there is a dual used for things normally associated in pairs and for the names of measures). For example:

sûs,	a horse	*sûsîm,*	horses
sûsâh,	a mare	*sûsôth,*	mares

True, not all nouns are so simple, and we do not wish to

pretend that Hebrew is as easy as Esperanto. The addition of
accented endings, -*îm*, -*âh*, -*ôth*, brings about in some cases
changes in the vowels of the stem, their shortening or disappearance. So:

gâdhôl, great	*gᵉdhôlâh* (f. sing.)	*gᵉdhôlîm* (m. pl.)
melek, king	*malkâh*, queen	*mᵉlâkhîm*, kings

Besides this, we also meet in Hebrew what the grammarians
call exceptions: masculines with feminine endings and *vice versa*
(cf. Latin *nauta*, masc., and *ficus*, fem.) and feminines of a
different form altogether from the masculine (Eng. *horse* and
mare). All this requires a stage of sheer learning by heart, which
is, however, soon passed.

There is the same simplicity about the article, which is used
rather more widely than the English definite article, like the
French. There is one form only for both genders and all numbers, *ha*, which is prefixed to its noun and causes the doubling
of its initial consonant:

sûs, a horse	*hassûs*, the horse
hassûsîm, the horses	*hassûsâh*, the mare

There are only two difficulties. The first concerns nouns
beginning with a guttural. In this case, to compensate for the
now impossible doubling of the initial consonant, the article
often has a long ä instead of the short a:

'âdhâm, a man	*hâ'âdhâm*, the man

The other occurs when one of the simple particles *lᵉ*, *bᵉ* or *kᵉ*
has to be joined to a noun with the definite article: the particle
and the article are combined, the *he* of the latter disappearing:

hassûs, the horse	*lassûs* (and not *lᵉhassûs*), to the horse
hâ'âdhâm, the man	*kâ'âdhâm*, like the man

On the whole, all this presents no real difficulty. There is in
the morphology and syntax of the noun one case only which is
interesting, that expressing the relation of possession.

THE CONSTRUCT STATE

We have said that there is not, or there is no longer, any genitive in Hebrew; that is, there is no case affecting the noun referring to the possessor (English apostrophe *s*, *Peter's book*, or the Latin *liber Petri*). Nor is there normally a preposition denoting possession (our *of*). The relation of possession is expressed by quite a different form of expression: the noun denoting the possessed and that denoting the possessor are written together in that order to form a sort of phonetic unit with one principal accent only, on the second word, the first partly losing its accent. To take the simplest example: "the king's horse" becomes *sûs hammelek*, literally "horse the king".

Now in Hebrew the loss of the accent on the first word, that denoting the possessed, causes it to assume very often a form different from that it normally has, a form in which certain of its vowels are shortened and, in appropriate cases, its ending modified. This is the form called the *construct state*, as opposed to the *absolute state*, the normal form. If the term declension may be used, we may speak of two cases in Hebrew, the construct and absolute states. These few examples may help to show how this works:

"the king's horse"—*sûs hammelek* (note that the construct state, being made determinate by the following noun, never has the article);

> the king's horses, *sûsê hammelek*;
> the king of Israel, *melek yisrâ'el*;
> the queen of Israel, *malkath yisrâ'el*.

So we get a typical "declension" like this, to take a fairly difficult word:

	masculine		feminine	
	sing.	*plur.*	*sing.*	*plur.*
absolute	melek	m^elâkhîm	malkâh	m^elâkhôth
construct	melek	malkê	malkath	malkôth

The form of the possessive adjective produces similar modifications of the noun as the construct state, being formed of a suffix added to the noun; these suffixes are fragmentary parts of the personal pronouns:

> my horse, *sûsî*
> his horse, *sûsô*
> your horse, *sûse̊khem*
> my king, *malkî*
> his king, *malkô*
> your king, *malke̊khem*
> my queen, *malkâthî*
> his queen, *malkâthô*
> your queen, *malkathkhem*

These forms are very characteristic of the Semitic languages, and have no precise parallels in our western idiom.[1] They are commonly used, replacing adjectives and various kinds of complements, and so give Hebrew a concrete and synthetic appearance which strikes the reader, even in translation.

---

[1] The English possessive case (*the boy's book*), compound words (*wine-bottle*), or the genitives of inflected languages, are none of them really analogous. In Hebrew the order possessed-possessor is always kept and it is the first of the two words which is modified.

CHAPTER IV

THE HEBREW VERB

ITS FORMS

The real singularity of Hebrew in western eyes is shown in its verbal system. It is at once remarkably rich and remarkably poor: it is rich in its power to express fine distinctions in the kind of action signified by the verb, poor in its inability to differentiate what we call tenses and moods. But fundamentally this represents a way of thinking very different from ours. This is why we must spend some time on the verb, not to introduce the reader to the mysteries of the grammar, but to enable him to understand an essential aspect of Hebrew thought.

We can take as our example the verb *qâṭal*, "to kill", which is a convenient one for paradigms though little used in Hebrew. In this one root there is the basis of three verbs with different senses: a *simple* verb, "kill"; an *intensive* verb, "to slaughter, destroy", and a *causative* verb, "to cause to kill". So, to take the third person singular of the perfect, which is the simplest form and the one used to designate the verb (as we use the infinitive), we get three possible forms:

qâṭal, he has killed; *qiṭṭel*, he has slaughtered; *hiqṭîl*, he has caused to kill.

Each of these forms may now be conjugated in the three voices, active, passive and reflexive (or middle), which theoretically gives nine possible forms for each verb root[1]:

	active	passive	reflexive
simple	*qâṭal*	←	*niqṭal*
intensive	*qiṭṭel*	*quṭṭal*	*hithqaṭṭel*
causative	*hiqṭîl*	*hoqṭal*	

[1] Each form has a name: the simple form is called *qal*, the "light" form. The others could be called by the third person singular of each, but they

Notice that there are only seven forms, for there is no causative reflexive, and the simple passive, if it existed, has disappeared and been replaced by the reflexive.[2] But it is very rare to find all these forms of any one root actually used; all Hebrew verbs are more or less defective.

As we have seen, verbal forms are differentiated by three modifications: duplication of one of the root consonants, the addition of preformatives and the change in the vocalization. These modifications are always the same; in other words, there is in Hebrew but one conjugation, properly speaking. So that given any verbal root one can easily make the various forms: from *kâthabh*, "to write", comes an intensive *kittebh*, a causative *hikhtîbh*, etc. The dictionary will always tell one which forms are used and what they mean.

Even the irregularities in the verb themselves follow precise phonetic rules and are therefore capable of being worked out from the root. They are generally due to the presence in the root either of a guttural, which has, among other characteristics, that of being impossible to double,[3] or of a weak letter, which causes modifications in the conjugation of the verb because of its tendency to lose its consonantal value.[4] These are not really "irregularities" at all, but forms which can be worked out since their causes can easily be understood. There is thus nothing

---

are generally known by the perfect of the ancient paradigm of *pâ'al*, "to act, do", so that the forms are called *niph'al, pi'el, pu'al, hiph'îl, hoph'al, hithpa'el*.

[2] The Hebrew verb is relatively poor in this regard when compared with that of the other Semitic languages, which have preserved many other forms.

[3] These are *guttural verbs*, distinguished, obviously, into three groups, according to which root consonant is the guttural.

[4] These are *weak verbs*, divided into various categories. The radical consonants of any verb are called, in order, its *pe*, its *'ayin* and its *lamedh*, from the three consonants of the paradigm verb *pa'al*. So weak verbs are divided into *pe-'aleph* and *pe-yodh* (the first consonant being an *'aleph* or a *yodh*), *'ayin-yodh* and *'ayin-waw* (the second consonant being a *yodh* or a *waw*), and *lamedh-'aleph* and *lamedh-he* (the third consonant being an *'aleph* or a *he*). Added to these are two slightly different categories, *pe-nun* verbs (the first letter being a *nun*, a consonant which is apt to be assimilated to the one following) and *double 'ayin* verbs, in which the second and third letters are the same (e.g. *gâlal*, "to roll").

3—S.L.

analogous to our English verbs which have forms from several different roots: "to be", "I am", "I was"; "I go", "I went".

Once these seven forms of the Hebrew verb are known conjugation is easy. There are two "tenses" of the "indicative" mood, an imperative, two forms of the infinitive and a participle. The two indicative tenses are generally called the *perfect* and the *imperfect*.[5] Here as an example is the simple conjugation of the perfect of *qâṭal*:

	singular	plural
3rd pers. masc.	qâṭal	qâṭᵉlû
— fem.	qâṭᵉlâh	
2nd pers. masc.	qâṭaltâ	qᵉṭaltem
— fem.	qâṭalt	qᵉṭalten
1st pers. com.	qâṭaltî	qâṭalnû

The conjugation of the imperfect is a little more complicated, as it is formed by the use of both preformatives and afformatives; so, the imperfect of *qâṭal* is:

	singular	plural
3rd pers. masc.	yiqṭôl	yiqṭᵉlû
— fem.	tiqṭôl	tiqṭôlnâh
2nd pers. masc.	tiqṭôl	tiqṭᵉlû
— fem.	tiqṭᵉlî	tiqṭôlnâh
1st pers. com.	'eqṭôl	niqṭôl

The student who knows these two tenses will then have no trouble in applying the rules to the other forms himself: *qiṭṭel, qiṭṭᵉlâh, qiṭṭaltâ, qiṭṭalt, qiṭṭaltî*, etc.; *hiqṭîl, hiqṭîlâh, hiqṭaltâ, hiqṭalt, hiqṭaltî*, etc. He has only to master certain techniques for forming the various parts of the verb, and for this some effort of the memory is needed. But it is all contained in the two pages of "The Regular Verb" to be found in any grammar. Anyone who knows those two pages thoroughly has weathered the worst part of learning Hebrew.

[5] Some grammarians call them the *past* and *future*, but it will be seen that this nomenclature is unfortunate.

ITS USE

The syntax of these forms will also provide a few surprises for the reader. It is fairly obvious that there can be no question of translating by these two "tenses" of Hebrew the various distinctions made in English, with our three moods, divided into three main tenses, past, present and future, these being further subdivided into imperfect, a present in the past, pluperfect, a past relative to another past time, future perfect, a past relative to the future, etc. Hebrew is incomparably simpler and does not know most of these differences: this must be accepted at the outset. But on the other hand it is possible to express in Hebrew distinctions not made in our modern languages, or which they can only render imperfectly by periphrases or by using adverbs. In short, we are dealing with a quite different way of thinking, and it would be dangerous to attempt to categorize Hebrew grammar in the terms of our modern western European mind.

The whole verbal system of Hebrew rests not on a distinction of *time*, of the tenses of the verb (past, present and future), but of its *state*. It expresses directly the completed ("perfect") character of the action or its incomplete ("imperfect") character, and indirectly some other aspects, instantaneous or lasting (durative) action, single or repeated and, lastly, the time or tense.

These distinctions are not, of course, altogether unknown in the western languages. We distinguish between "I saw" and "I have seen": "I saw" is instantaneous, with no indication of the moment of time or of my present state, whereas "I have seen" is precisely a description of my present state; similar distinctions are made in "the man died", "the man has died", "the man is dead", "the man has been dead for two years". Analogous differences are expressed in some passives: "the door is shut" and "the door has been shut" and "the door is being shut" (cf. German: *die Tür ist geschlossen* and *die Tür wird geschlossen*). These few examples, which it would be easy to multiply,[6] have been given with no other purpose than to make the complications of the Semitic verb seem less disconcerting.

So in Hebrew the first idea expressed by the perfect is that of an action completed at the time the words are spoken: *kâthabh*, "he had written", "he has written", "he will have written". The basic idea of the imperfect is that of uncompleted action: *yikhtôbh*, "he was writing", "he is writing", "he will write". But the idea of completion carries with it that of rapidity, and so of instantaneousness and uniqueness: so *kâthabh* takes on the meaning "he has written quickly" or "once only", while *yikhtôbh* means, according to the context, "he was writing . . . he is writing . . . continuously or frequently". Lastly, the "finished" (*perfectum*) is most often expressed as a past, while the unfinished, what is still going on or will be finished later, tends to be considered rather as a present or future. So there are introduced into Hebrew the time-differences which, while they are not primitive, yet, since they are so very useful in narrative, tend to leave unheeded the aspect or state of the verb. The perfect *kâthabh* so comes to mean "he wrote" and *yikhtôbh*, "he will write", irrespective of the complete or incomplete character of the action.

This is what has led some grammarians to speak of a "past" and a "future" rather than of a "perfect" and an "imperfect". This is unfortunate in so far as it unduly assimilates the conjugation of the Hebrew verb to that of our own tongues, and also in that it appears to ignore the state, the kind of action denoted, which is so characteristic of Hebrew. And indeed on every page of good, classical Hebrew prose examples can be found to contradict this terminology. "Thus did (*yaʻªseh*, imperfect) Job every day" (Job 1. 5); "Here thou mayest eat thy fill and bless the name of the Lord thy God for the fair land he has given (i.e. will have given, *nâthan*, perfect) thee" (Deut. 8. 10). If the words are still to mean anything we cannot speak of a

---

[6] For example, by quoting the Greek aorist and perfect, or by going to the Slavonic languages, so well provided with the means to express these sorts of aspects of the verb.

"future" in the first case or of a "past" in the second. The terms "perfect" and "imperfect" are still the most apt for the Hebrew tenses.

But this is not all: there are still the Hebrew moods.

There is nothing that needs to be said about the *optative* mood, that concerned with the expression of the speaker's will. It comprises: in the second person, the imperative; in the third, the jussive ("let him write"); and in the first, the cohortative ("let me, us write"). The forms are not very different from those of the indicative; and the system is clearly more complete than in most languages.

The *consecutive mood* is much more important; it is very common and its use is somewhat tricky. The form of the verb has no parallel in English, though the use of the conjunction has analogies. An idea of result or consecution, that is, of immediate succession, sometimes accompanied by logical consequence, is added to the verb's significance of aspect and time; so in "he went out and met his father" or "he will go out and meet his father", for the second verb in each case the consecutive mood is used in Hebrew. Now, though it may seem odd, to express consecution on a verb in the perfect the *imperfect* is normally used, sometimes accented and vocalized differently, always first in its phrase and introduced by the conjunction "and" with the vocalization of the article (*wa* and not *we*), which causes the duplication of the initial consonant of the verb: "and he killed", *wayyiqtôl*. On the other hand, to express consecution on a first verb in the imperfect, the *perfect* is used, sometimes accented differently, always first in its clause, and introduced by the normal conjunction (*we*): "and he will kill", *weqâtal*.

The use of the tenses in the consecutive mood is thus the inverse of their normal usage: perfect where the imperfect would have been used, imperfect where one would have used the perfect. For this reason some grammarians have called this mood *conversive* or *inversive* and the tenses *converted* or *inverted*.

There follow some examples which will show something of

the workings of the consecutive mood and of the Hebrew verb generally:

Gen. 3. 17: "And to Adam he said (*'âmar*, perfect): because you have listened to (*shâma'tâ*, perfect) your wife's counsel, and have eaten (*wattô'khal*, consec. imperf.) of the tree of which I commanded you (*siwwîthî*, perf.), saying: you shall not eat of it (*thô'khal*, imperf.) . . ."

Gen. 4. 1: "And Adam knew (*yâdha'*, perf.) Eve his wife, and she conceived (*wattahar*, consec. imperf.), and bore (*watteledh*, id.) Cain, and she said (*wattô'mer*, id.), I have got (*qânîthî*, perf.) . . ."

Gen. 31. 33–4: "Then he went out of (*wayyeçe'*, consec. imperf.) Lia's tent and went into (*wayyâbhô'*, id.) Rachel's. Now Rachel had taken (*lâq^eḥâh*, perf.) . . ."

Deut. 8. 10: "And you will eat (*w^e'âkhaltâ*, consec. perf.) and be filled (*w^esâbhâ'tâ*, id.) and will bless (*ûbherakhtâ*, id.) Yahweh your God for the good land which he will have given you (*nâthan*, perf.)."

1 Sam. 16. 2–3: "And Yahweh said (*wayyô'mer*, consec. imperf.): you will take (*tiqqaḥ*, imperf.) a heifer and you will say (*w^e'âmartâ*, consec. perf.): I have come (*bâ'thî*, perf.) to sacrifice to Yahweh. And you will invite (*w^eqârâ'thâ*, consec. perf.) Jesse to the sacrifice and I will show you (*'ôdhî'akhâ*, imperf.) all that you will (i.e. shall, must) do (*ta'aseh*, imperf.)." [7]

It can be seen how easy it is to mix up indicative and consecutive forms in one period, and how in particular the writers of Israel like to break a series of consecutive tenses to revert to an indicative, so as to mark in this way that there was no consecution. In particular this was the way in which they generally rendered what we call pluperfects and "conditionals", or the future in the past ("he said that he *would come*").

These constructions allow of the achievement of some great

---

[7] It will be seen from these last three examples that the first, non-consecutive, verb can be "understood"; there are sentences, chapters, even whole books which begin with a consecutive imperfect, which practically became (in later books) a simple past definite.

stylistic effects. They demand of the exegete some serious analysis and careful thinking. Translation is quite a different thing from mechanical transposition, which is too often found in both ancient and modern versions.

To end this grammatical summary a word only must be said of the infinitive mood. As in all languages, the participle is a sort of verbal adjective; it serves therefore to denote a prolonged state or action without any indication of time. It is frequently used in circumstantial clauses (often with '*ôdh*, "still, yet") and after "behold", *hinneh*, with the verb *to be* understood, and it particularly expresses continuousness, equivalent to the English *to be* with the present participle, which is unsatisfactorily rendered by the personal tenses. E.g. Gen. 9. 9: "Behold, I establish my covenant with you . . .", literally, "Behold me establishing . . ." (*meqîm*).

The infinitive is a verbal noun; in Hebrew it has two forms. The *construct infinitive* is more or less equivalent to the English infinitive. With a preposition it makes a kind of gerund (*le'môr*, "in saying"). The *absolute infinitive* has one use of special interest: put before or, more often, after a finite verb with the same root it strengthens or modifies the meaning; Gen. 2. 17: "thou shalt surely die", *môth tâmûth*, lit., "dying thou shalt die"; Gen. 3. 16: "I will greatly multiply thy sorrow", *harbâh 'arbeh*, lit., "multiplying I will multiply". Sometimes even an infinitive from a different root will affect a finite verb as if it were an adverb. A characteristic example of this is the infinitive *hashkem* which, after a long process of semantic evolution, came to mean "early in the morning".[8]

Such are the most characteristic features of Hebrew grammar. The picture is not, of course, complete; it has never claimed to be. A more serious disadvantage is that a summary of this kind

[8] The nominal root *shekhem* means "shoulder", whence the verb *shâkham*, which, in the causative form *hishkîm*, means "to put on the shoulder" and so "to load"; since the loading of beasts of burden was done early in the morning before setting out, it came to mean "to do something early in the morning", and the infinitive, used adverbially, *hashkem*, "early in the morning".

can hardly do more than explain techniques or describe forms; it reveals very little of the living thought that made and used them. This is only to say that a grammatical summary can only be an introduction to the reading of the Scriptures; nothing can make direct contact with the text unnecessary. There only will be found "the Hebrew mind" and the thought of the Bible in all its richness and variety.

CHAPTER V

NOTES ON HEBREW STYLE

It has for long been recognized that the ancient Semites had little taste for abstract thought. The greater their poetic gifts, the more foreign to them philosophic thinking seems to be. Now the character of the people being such, it may be expected to show itself to some degree in the structure of the language.

But this is just where we cannot trust the translations. For the translator, who cannot be content with a simple word for word version and who is forced, simply by the nature of the languages concerned, to permit himself some freedom in transposing ideas, is often led to render what is concrete by an abstraction, at the risk of obscuring one of the essential characteristics of the original text.

Everyone can quote the beginning of Ecclesiastes: "Vanity of vanities, saith the Preacher, vanity of vanities; all is vanity." In English, as in Latin and Greek, the thought seems quite abstract. But the word used in Hebrew, *hebhel*, means "breath", "exhalation", "damp", "dust" or "wind"; and probably the image was still felt, as was that of "striving for the wind" (*re'ûth rûaḥ*) which is used with it in v. 14.

In Hebrew, real abstracts are rare, and even those are used infrequently, especially in the classical period, and are often replaced by concrete plurals, for example. To say "perversity", *tahpukhôth*, "perverse things", was used; *baṭṭuḥôth*, "safety", and *mêshârîm*, "uprightness", are similar plurals. To these we can add plural words denoting age: *behûrôth*, "youth", *zequnîm*, "old age", *ne'ûrîm*, "unmarried boyhood or girlhood", etc. Lastly, the word *derek* really ought to have a separate study devoted to it. Its primary sense is "way, road", but from that it came to mean "way of behaving", and so "manner of life" or "conduct", or "way of thinking" (cf. Ezech. 18. 29 ff.; 33. 17 ff.). The image is found often in the Psalms and in the New Testament (where it had the same meaning). But in many passages in the oldest writings the metaphor still seems to have been felt as such, and a good translation ought perhaps to make this evident (cf. Prov. 30. 19).

The same might be said of the word *rûaḥ*, frequently translated, and rightly, "spirit". But its primary sense is "wind, breath".[1] In several texts the author seems to be signifying two ideas at once, which makes the task of the translator unusually difficult. In Gen. 2. 7, did God breathe into man "the breath of life" or "the spirit of life"? Did Ezechiel call down on the dry bones (37. 5) the "breath" or the "spirit" of the Lord? In the same way it is never clear whether we ought to speak of "the spirit" or "the Spirit". This richness of meaning is also found in the New Testament: Jesus speaks to Nicodemus of the Spirit which "breathes where it will" (John 3. 8), and some interpreters have supposed that at that moment the sound of the wind was heard outside as if to emphasize the words.[2]

As much could be said of *nephesh*, which means "throat", and so "breath", and thence "desire", "life" and "soul". In certain contexts it means "self", "person", and so can replace the reflexive pronoun: "to love one's soul" is "to love oneself"; "to save one's soul" could mean "to save oneself" or "to save one's life". But these distinctions are obviously fine ones: the translator must guard against a double danger, of lessening the moral or theological content of a text, and of interpreting it anachronistically.

With this poverty of Hebrew in the realm of abstracts we can associate its distaste, almost, for adjectives. True, they are

[1] Like the Latin *antmus*; but this word very early developed its abstract meaning while the corresponding Greek word ἄνεμος kept the meaning "wind" (as distinct from πνεῦμα).

[2] Others think that Jesus was using a commonplace expression, a sort of proverb understood by all; but do not forget that the saying is reported by St John. (See note *ad loc.* in Knox version.)

not completely lacking: in Hebrew as in all languages we can say "great", *gadhôl*; "small", *qâṭôn*; "heavy", *kâbhedh*; "wise", *hâkhâm*; etc. But it is none the less true that the adjective, even when there is one, is often replaced by a different mode of expression, particularly when it is attributive: "the seed of royalty", *zera' hammᵉlukhâh* (4 Kings 25. 25), for "royal blood"; "the place of holiness", *mᵉqôm haqqôdhesh* (Lev. 14. 13), for "holy ground"; "kings of mercy", *malkê ḥesedh* (3 Kings 20. 31), for "merciful kings"; and even "house of eternity", *bêyth 'ôlâm* (Eccles. 12. 5), for "eternal home" (the grave). One might think that the words of Matt. 24. 15, "the abomination of desolation", borrowed from the Greek of Daniel 9. 27 (cf. 11. 31; 12. 11), correspond to an idiom of this kind. But the Hebrew of Daniel in these passages has a different construction, with a participle. Either the Greek translator of Daniel had a different text, or he himself rendered by a Hebraism in his Greek a less characteristic construction in his original.

While we are speaking of the paucity of Hebrew adjectives, we might mention a real lack of means to express the degrees of comparison. Hebrew has no comparative forms; the idea is expressed not by a change in the form of the adjective, but only by one construction, indicating comparison: e.g. "greater than all the people" becomes "good as-distinct-from (*min*) all the people"; "more numerous than the sand of the sea" becomes "numerous more-than (*min*) the sands of the sea". When, however, the standard of comparison is not expressed, nor is the comparison itself: "Cry louder" (3 Kings 18. 27), is actually "cry loudly", and only the context suggests the comparison. The Vulgate has often handed on such comparisons translated literally: Ps. 117. 9, *bonum est sperare in Domino quam sperare in principibus*. Sometimes the translator has tried to express the comparison more clearly: Ps. 118. 72, *bonum mihi lex oris tui super millia auri*. . . . The New Testament also has sometimes preserved Hebraisms of this kind: so Mark 9. 42 (43 in the Greek) has literally: "It is good for you to enter into life lame, (rather) than. . . ."

The difficulty is greater and the solutions more various in the

case of the relative superlative.[3] Sometimes Hebrew uses
repetition: it seems probable that the triple *sanctus* of Isaias 6. 3
corresponds to a kind of emphatic superlative (in some other
texts, Jer. 7. 4; Ezech. 21. 32, it is a noun which is emphasized
and repeated in this way). Sometimes a genitival construction is
used: the "Holy of holies", *qôdhesh haqqodhâshîm*; the "Song of
songs", *shîr hashshîrîm*, that is, the perfect Song. But for the
most part Hebrew makes do with the positive adjective made
definite by the article: "the young one of his sons", *qᵉtôn
bânâyîm* (2 Paralip. 21. 17), for "the youngest of his sons";
"from the great to the small", *miggᵉdhôlâm wᵉ'adh-qᵉtonnâm*
(Jonas 3. 5), for "from the greatest to the least"; *hayyâphâh
bannâshîm*, "the fair among women" (Cant. 1. 8), for "fairest
among women". The words used by the angel addressing Mary
(Luke 1. 28; cf. Elizabeth's words, 42), "blessed art thou
among women" (Greek ἐν, "in"; Latin *benedicta tu* in *mulieribus*)
—that is, "most blessed among women"—are thus a Hebraism
used for a superlative.

The adverb also is rare in Hebrew. The various, compara-
tively simple, ways of replacing it by adverbial phrases or
predicative adjectives are known to most languages, but
Hebrew has some more subtle constructions of its own. We have
already mentioned (p. 39) the use of the infinitive to strengthen
or modify the meaning of a verb. This is one of the Hebraisms
most commonly met with in the translations: *morte morieris*,
Gen. 2. 17; *plorans ploravit*, Lam. 1. 2; *euntes ibant . . .
venientes autem venient*, Ps. 125. 6; *castigans castigavit me
Dominus*, Ps. 117. 18. The text of Luke 22. 15 would lead one
to suppose a similar expression lay behind it: *desiderio desideravi*;
but Jesus was certainly not speaking Hebrew, and the construction is unknown in Aramaic. Aramaic does, however, have
an internal accusative, the use of a noun strengthening the sense
of a verb with the same root, and this is exactly the form
suggested by Luke.

[3] There is no difficulty with the absolute superlative (Eng., "very . . .",
as distinct from "most . . ."), as the adverb *mᵉ'ôdh* is used, put after the
adjective (Latin *valde* or *nimis*).

Another idiom, sometimes badly rendered by the translations, is the use of verbs as quasi-auxiliaries. To translate the English adverb "again", to mark the repetition of an action, the verb *shûbh*, "to return", is used in Hebrew, coordinated with another verb. So Gen. 26. 18: "he dug again", *wayyâshâbh . . . wayyaḥpôr*, lit., "he returned and he dug"; Isaias 6. 13: "it will be destroyed again", *wᵉshâbhâh wᵉhâyᵉthâh lᵉbhâ'êr*, lit., "it will return and will be destroyed".

Such constructions leave room sometimes for doubt; should one give the verb *shûbh* its full meaning, "to return, to turn back", or think of it as an auxiliary? Isaias 6. 10 is usually translated "so that they cannot . . . turn back to me and win healing", but grammatically the Hebrew words, *wâshâbh wᵉrâphâ*, could simply mean ". . . be healed again". In other cases the sense is clear: 4 Kings 21. 3 is thus translated by the Vulgate: "he (Manasses) turned again and constructed the hill-shrines", which is odd, to say the least; in fact, the text, *wayyâshâbh wayyibhen*, means "he restored".

The verb *yâṣaph*, "to add", has an analogous use, with the meaning "still", marking the continuation of an action: Gen. 25. 1, "Abraham again took a wife", *wayyôṣeph 'abrâhâm wayyiqqaḥ*, lit., "Abraham added and took . . ."

It is sometimes said that Hebrew cannot express subordination, but can only set propositions alongside of one another. This is much exaggerated. There are in Hebrew, as in all languages of civilized peoples, subordinating conjunctions: 'because, since", *kî, 'asher*; "lest", *pen*; "if", *'im, lû*; "unless", *lûle*'; and the compound conjunctions: "because, since", *ya'an'asher*; "in order that", *lᵉma'an 'asher*; "according as", *ka'asher*; etc.

Nevertheless, it is true that instead of expressing subordination clearly, Hebrew prefers to use less definite constructions with simple coordinating conjunctions. The reader has to fill in this vagueness and supply the shade of meaning suggested by the context. E.g.:

Gen. 7. 6: "He (Noe) was six hundred years old when the waters of the flood covered the earth" (lit., "and the waters . . .").

Gen. 18. 13: "Am I to bear a child although I am old?" (lit., "and I am old").

Jer. 29. 31: "Because Semeias prophesied against you, when I had not sent him" (lit., "and I had not sent him").

Clearly in all such cases the task of the translator is a delicate one. He must watch for two mistakes: on the one hand he must not improperly westernize the Bible by expressing with a wealth of subordinate clauses what the original tongue deliberately left vague; on the other hand he must avoid making Hebrew seem a "primitive" or "childlike" language incapable of conceiving other grammatical relations than simple parataxis. Without being as closely knit as Greek or Latin, or even modern English, Hebrew can follow and express the normal processes of our thinking. But it does so in ways generally more subtle than our own; it is for the translator to grasp and transmit this subtlety.

These have only been examples chosen more or less at random and designed simply to give the reader his bearings. Too many teachers, obsessed by the difficulties of phonetics and morphology, do not dwell on what constitutes the particular interest of Hebrew. We can only advise the young student to give his whole attention to those aspects of syntax and style peculiar to Hebrew. In that way he will see that Hebrew has its own character, its own subtlety and its own difficulties. This calls for the student's industry, it is true, but also for his intelligence and for some hard thinking. This is not said to discourage him, but so that he may the better prepare himself for the business of learning Hebrew.

CHAPTER VI

HEBREW LITERATURE

For a long time ancient Hebrew literature was only known in the Biblical writings. But since the end of the last century archeological discoveries have revealed to us a number of Hebrew documents enabling us to complete to some extent our knowledge of the language. Besides, the use of Hebrew was continued in Judaism long after the Bible was made, to give birth to a flourishing literature.

So it is best to present Hebrew literature under three heads: Ancient documents other than the Bible; Biblical literature; and Post-Biblical Jewish literature.

DOCUMENTS OTHER THAN THE BIBLE

The most ancient evidence for the language of Canaan, before the Hebrews settled in Palestine, is in the tablets from Tell el Amarna. True, these are letters of the fourteenth century B.C., written in Assyro-Babylonian, the diplomatic language of the age, but they are not only influenced by the language of the country in which they were written but are provided with explanatory glosses in the Canaanite tongue, themselves written in cuneiform script. A careful analysis of these documents has enabled scholars to reconstruct certain aspects of the language spoken in Canaan on the eve of the Israelite invasion.[1]

If we leave aside the "calendar of Gezer", which is difficult to interpret as well as to date (ninth century?), the oldest remains of Hebrew are inscriptions.

[1] See *Recueil Edouard Dhorme* (Paris 1951), pp. 405-87: La langue de Canaan.

We have some hesitation in mentioning the Moabite stone,[2] discovered to the east of the Jordan and erected by a king of Moab to celebrate his achievements in the ninth century. But since we have, besides this text, neither inscriptions nor literature in the Moabite tongue, and since moreover the differences between Moabite and Hebrew are few and unimportant, we can regard it more or less as a dialect of Hebrew and simply include the Moabite stone in an account of Hebrew literature.

The Siloam inscription,[3] of about a century later, is originally from Jerusalem and is written in a fine archaic script in pure Hebrew. Its few lines commemorate the piercing, under Ezechias, of a tunnel dug in the rock to join the spring in the valley of Ge-hinnom, on the eastern slope of the hill of Ophel, to the pool of Siloam to the south. Despite several technical terms it is a relatively easy text to understand.

We might also mention a number of minor pieces of epigraphic material: inscriptions on spearheads (going back perhaps to the twelfth century), on pots, seals and weights. But these generally consist of only two or three words, of great worth in the history of the script, but disappointing from the literary or linguistic point of view.

Quite a different kind of document is the ostracon, an ordinary potsherd covered with writing in ink made with a pen.

The oldest, found in the old city of Jerusalem, are practically indecipherable. The Samarian ostraca, several dozens in number, are simple little labels made to mark the taxes or services in kind received by the royal functionaries of the ninth and eighth centuries. For the most part they carry proper names and information of little linguistic interest; but these are the first readable evidence of a Hebrew script that is already cursive, which supposes a long tradition of writing among the scribes.

The important ostraca of Lachis must be mentioned for the sixth century; about twenty of them were found in 1935 at Tell ed Duweir, but only five were decipherable. One of these has a

[2] Discovered in 1868 and now in the Louvre.
[3] Discovered in 1880 and now in the Istanbul Museum; but there is in the Louvre a good cast made while the inscription was still in situ.

list of proper names; the others are private letters concerning contemporary events which it is not always easy to identify. From their contents, their script and their style, we can see that their authors were masters of the art of writing. As the works of Jeremias (ch. 36) and Ezechiel (ch. 2), near contemporaries, also show, we have already reached a period of literate civilization.

During the centuries that followed the Exile it seems that the art of the inscriptions suffered an eclipse. The records themselves, doubtless entrusted to materials too fragile to survive, have not come down to us; but in the realm of literature it was an age of great fruitfulness.

BIBLICAL LITERATURE

The literature of the Bible covers nearly ten centuries and fills over forty Hebrew books.[4] A good part of this literature was created in an age when the development of the language was not yet restrained by rules of literary usage, so these books ought to provide a remarkable picture of the evolution of the language and of the literature over the centuries.

But account must also be taken of certain factors working in the opposite sense. Firstly, several of these books are difficult to date; others are the end-products of complicated histories, and the various levels of revision and editing into which they seem divisible cannot all be treated in the same way. Lastly, the oldest among them were not preserved in their primitive state: when they were recopied the scribe was not averse from making them more modern and consistent, or from removing archaisms and provincialisms and anything else that might put off the contemporary reader. Later, it is true, as the sacred character of these books received greater recognition, there was less of this bringing up to date; but then the inverse phenomenon appeared: the books now canonical became a model which was more or less consciously to be imitated. The last books stuck

[4] Cf. in this series: *What is the Bible?* by Daniel-Rops, and the following volumes in the same section VI, "The Word of God". We are here only concerned to look at the literature from a linguistic point of view.

4—S.L.

faithfully to the established forms of the past, and were plainly out of date as compared with the evolving popular tongue. This is not to say that no difference is to be discerned between the oldest and the latest of the books of the Bible; but these differences do not extend beyond a certain narrow range, and give only an incomplete picture of the actual evolution of the language.

In spite of all this, scholars are agreed in distinguishing three elements: those clearly archaic, the great classical books and those held to be more recent.

The archaic elements are generally short poetic passages, poetry being always more conservative in its language and less amenable to alteration to bring it up to date. Everyone knows and can quote the song of Debbora (Judges 5), that wonderful epic hymn in such very difficult language. But we could also mention some elements of the prophecy of Jacob (Gen. 49), the prophecy of Balaam (Num. 23), the brief extract from the "Book of the Upright" in Josue (10. 12), the song of Lamech (Gen. 4. 23–4), etc.

The great classical books are: Isaias, who is universally recognized as the greatest writer of Israel, and his contemporary prophets Osee, Amos, Michaeas; also the other prophets down to the Exile, Jeremias, Ezechiel, Deutero-Isaias and several minor prophets. To this category also belong the ancient narratives of the Pentateuch and the deuteronomical writings, Deuteronomy and part of our historical books; and lastly, a good part of the Book of Proverbs and of the Psalms. True, there are differences between these various writings, but all together they represent the golden age of Hebrew, the time during which, made into a flexible instrument by the work of the great prophets, it was almost free from foreign influence.

After the Exile signs of decadence gradually appear. The most obvious is the influence of Aramaic. If Job was still written in a fine, nearly classical Hebrew, the foreign influence becomes increasingly evident with Ecclesiastes, Esther, some of the Psalms, Chronicles and the Hebrew text of Ecclesiasticus.

To this literature which is properly called Biblical we may

add the many apocryphal writings which flourished just before and at the beginning of the Christian era; that is, immediately after the canon of the Jewish Scriptures was closed. Such are the Book of Jubilees, the Testament of the Twelve Patriarchs, the Assumption of Moses, the Psalms of Solomon, etc.[5] Unfortunately, these books have only survived in translations, most often made by Christians. Except for a few tiny fragments recently discovered, the original text has been lost. In the case of several of them it is still a matter of discussion whether their original was Hebrew or Aramaic.

To the same period belong the writings produced by the sect of the Essenes, most of which have recently been published: The *Manual of Discipline* (or Rule of the Community), the symbolical story of the *War of the Sons of Light with the Sons of Darkness*, the *Damascus Document*, the *Thanksgiving Scroll*, a *Commentary on Habacuc* and some other fragments of commentaries on parts of the Bible. These numerous texts give us a very good idea of the state of the Hebrew language during the first century B.C.

POST-BIBLICAL JEWISH LITERATURE

After the destruction of Jerusalem and the triumph of Christianity, Hebrew did not disappear but was maintained as the inalienable heritage of the Jewish race.

It had, however, to put up a hard fight against some redoubtable challengers: first Aramaic, then Arabic and the western languages. Nor did it always emerge victorious; or, rather, it knew two sorts of defeat. At times it was frankly beaten; that is, abandoned in favour of its rivals. Thus several of the most important works of Judaism were written in Aramaic (a considerable portion of the Talmuds; the Book of Zohar) or in Arabic (the works of the medieval Jewish scholars and philosophers); to be compensated later, since all these books were translated into and most often preserved in Hebrew. At other times, without being so clearly defeated, Hebrew had

[5] See the Volume in this series dealing with Old Testament apocrypha.

to yield other languages important concessions: in order to maintain itself it had to borrow from them a good part of their vocabulary and structure. So was made Neo-Hebrew or, better, Middle Hebrew, to distinguish it from the language spoken in the State of Israel.

In the early years of the general dispersion of Israel Jewish literature took a peculiar turn: it was first and foremost a matter of making permanent in writing the oral teachings, already widely diffused, of the Pharisees, and represented by the great rabbis of the first two centuries. At first, doubtless, various collections were made of rabbinical sayings, but these were almost all replaced by or absorbed in the compilation of Rabbi Jehuda ha-Nasi known as the *Mishnah* ("Repetition"). The Mishnah was still written in Hebrew, but in a Hebrew much affected by Aramaic. With foreign words and new forms, infrequent use of the article, the progressive disappearance of the construct state and of the consecutive forms of the verb, Hebrew was gradually losing its most characteristic features.

But the Mishnah had not collected together all the sayings of the rabbis. It was therefore necessary to make another collection, the *Tosephta* ("addition"), less official, less fixed in its contents, a little later in date, but of a similar kind.

During the centuries that followed the Mishnah became the basis of teaching and was in turn commented on by the rabbis. From this came the Talmud, made up of two elements, the Mishnah, which supplied the form and substance of the book, and the *Gemara* ("Completion"), the commentary. But it is now no longer a matter of Hebrew literature: if the Mishnah, the basic text, was in Hebrew, the commentary was split between Hebrew and Aramaic, according to the age and origin of the sayings it embodied, but with a clear preponderance of Aramaic.

Beside this more or less official memorial of Judaism we must mention the *Midrashim* which appeared about the same time and went on being developed right into the Middle Ages. The Midrash was a Biblical commentary; the most ancient, *sifra* (on Leviticus), *sifre* (on Numbers and Deuteronomy) and *mechilta* (on Exodus), are made up mostly of the *halakhah*, that is, detailed precepts of the law. As such, they are related to the oldest parts of the Talmud. But the later Midrashim, which were many and of various dates about which it is often difficult to be precise, give place to the *haggadah*, the more or less legendary tale, to the marvellous and to eschatological speculation. In all this there are elements going back even to the time of Christ, and these are of the greatest interest; but it requires a good deal of shrewdness and patience to disentangle the ramifications of this mass of literature.

From the beginning of the eighth century Jewish literature was greatly influenced by contact with Arabic thought and later with the western world. More than ever before, Judaism was riven by the terrible choice, integrity or assimilation. There can be no question of setting out here, even briefly, the history of Jewish literature.[6] To conclude it will be sufficient to indicate the chief movements and mention the best-known names.

For those who held out for the integrity of Judaism the essential study was that of the Bible. More than this, the Caraites, those "Protestants of Judaism", would have liked to recognize in it an exclusive authority, and to reject the whole rabbinical tradition. Not everyone followed them, but all were agreed in making the sacred text the object of their care and attention. We have already spoken (p. 21) of the Massoretes and their work of editorship. They reached their height in the tenth century with ben Asher and ben Nephtali, who dispute the honour of providing Judaism with its official text of the Bible; ben Asher won because of the support he received from Maimonides.

A little later the study of Hebrew grammar developed, under the influence of Arabic science, with Abraham ibn Ezra (1092–1167) and then, especially, with the Qimhi, father and son (cf. p. 15).

As for Biblical exegesis, it was not only represented by the many haggadic midrashim; exegesis proper was equally practised

6 We can only refer the reader to the general works cited in the Bibliography, especially that of A. Waxman.

as a specialist study in the west, for example by Rabbi Salomon ben Isaac ("Rashi"), of Troyes (1040–1105), the prince of Jewish exegesis.

Rashi was also a commentator on the Talmud. He began the movement which, on the model of the *summae* of the scholastics, was to try, by careful and learned compilation, to bring some order into the vast Talmudic material. He was followed in this task by men like Rabbi Asher ben Jehiel ("Rosh") and his son Jacob ben Asher, the author of *Arba' Ṭurîm* ("the four orders"), and, much later, Joseph Caro (sixteenth century), the writer of *Shulḥân 'Arûk* ("the spread table"), the most complete *summa* of Jewish learning.

As against these Talmudists, generally loyal to Hebrew, and more or less rigid opponents of western science and philosophy, we must mention the scholars and philosophers. Everyone knows of Salomon ben Jehudah ibn Gebirol, Avicebron, as he was called in the west. It is true that his *Fountain of Life* was written in Arabic, but the original has been lost; the work is preserved in the Hebrew translation, *Meqôr ḥayyim*, which was in its turn translated into Latin (*Fons vitae*) and had a great influence in the Middle Ages. Moses ben Maimon, or Maimonides, was the greatest Jewish thinker. Born at Cordova in 1135, he died in Old Cairo in 1204; he was a doctor, a disciple of Galen; a Talmudist of repute, a diligent reader of Aristotle. He tried to make a synthesis, which was impossible, of traditional Judaism, Jewish mysticism and certain elements of Greek rationalism. His *Guide to the Perplexed*, written in Arabic and translated into Hebrew (*Môrê Nebûkhîm*), tries to reconcile revelation and reason, theology and philosophy. He was the cause of much discussion in Judaism, but represents an important movement which was to end in the theoretical justifiers of assimilation, and to find its most illustrious representative in the eighteenth century in Moses Mendelsohn.

It has been said that the ghetto has no poetry. How wrong! But that too hesitates between traditionalism and modernism. Beside the many liturgical poems, the *piyyutîm* (transcription of the Greek ποιητής), most often anonymous, which were produced from Byzantine to medieval times, we have also philosophical poetry, represented by Avicebron. With Jehudah ben Samuel hal-Lewi (1085–1140), a doctor from Cordova, friendship, love, human fate, all the themes, in short, of Arabic poetry, come into Jewish poetry. At the same time, in the wonderful "Songs of Sion" of the same poet is expressed all the nostalgic "Sionism" of the Middle Ages.

But the highest flight of the Jewish soul was in mysticism. This tradition goes back a very long way, to the apocalyptic prophets, to the Midrashim and the Talmud, which includes many more or less esoteric ideas. Right through the Middle Ages we can follow the unbroken stream of Jewish mysticism, in works very little known in the west.[7] The compilation in which all this culminated, the famous *Zohar* (Splendour), is an Aramaic work (cf. p. 68); but it cannot be passed by in silence here, because of its enormous influence among the Jews (especially the sect of the Hasidim) and even among the Christians also (Pico della Mirandola; Reuchlin).

Far from the history of Jewish literature breaking off, it has seen in our own days a real renaissance. We are not now going to launch out into the story of Israeli literature; but let us at least salute its remarkable success with understanding and deep feeling. That a language dead for more than twenty centuries should be shocked into life by such an apostle as Eliezer ben Jehuda (Perelmann) to become again the language of a people is already a sort of miracle. But we can wonder still more at this national literature's rich variety, which is at once the consequence and the most striking evidence of Hebrew's resurrection.

[7] See the outstanding account by G. G. Scholem: *Major Trends in Jewish Mysticism* (H. S. Stroock Lectures, 1938), Jerusalem, 1941, and New York, Schocken Books.

CHAPTER VII

ARAMAIC: THE LANGUAGE

It is sometimes said that Aramaic is a corrupt Hebrew, a sort of degenerate country dialect which the Jews brought back from the Babylonian captivity. From a historical as well as from a linguistic point of view, such a statement is indefensible. The truth is that Aramaic spread gradually all over the Near East, and this peaceful invasion, which started in the time of the Aramaic kingdoms, almost coincided, so far as concerns the land of Judah, with the period of Persian domination. Aramaic is not a decadent Hebrew, but an independent language like Hebrew, more archaic in some respects, but clearly further evolved in others.

Aramaic is a Semitic language, like Hebrew, Accadian or Arabic. It belongs to the north-western group [1] and consequently most resembles Hebrew and Phoenician. But these languages are separated by clear differences. If a modern parallel is needed, the relationship between Hebrew and Aramaic is roughly that between French and Italian.

At first Aramaic was the language of the nomadic tribes which, during the second millennium B.C., invaded in successive waves not only Upper Mesopotamia and Syria, but also, under the name of Chaldaeans, a good part of Babylonia. In this way they created a number of small states, more or less ephemeral, especially in the north-west: Aram-Rehob, Aram-Zobah, Aram-Maachah, Aram-Hamath, etc. Only the state of Damascus was able to keep itself in being; it was a prosperous state down to its destruction by Tiglath-Pileser III of Assyria in 734 B.C.

[1] See the table of Semitic languages, pp. 13–14.

But after the disappearance of these kingdoms Aramaic, far from falling into oblivion, survived as the *lingua franca* of the region. At first used for trade and dealings between states, it spread in the diplomatic world, especially in the time of the Babylonian empire, founded by the Chaldaeans. During the period of the Persian empire it became a kind of common language for the whole Near East. But since it was spoken in all kinds of countries, and had neither a native, national state to preserve its unity, nor a literature to ensure the preponderance of one dialect over the others, Aramaic was bound to end by splitting into two distinct dialects, eastern and western Aramaic.

But this split was slow and late in developing. It was in fact the common Aramaic which was introduced into Palestine under the Persians and which lasted until the beginning of the Christian era. So it is to that common Aramaic that our oldest Aramaic literary remains belong, two largish fragments in our Bibles, Esdras 4. 8—6. 18; 7. 12–26 and Daniel 2. 4b—7. 28. It is this "Old Testament Aramaic", a sacred language for the Christian, that is dealt with in the few pages that follow.

ARAMAIC SCRIPT

Aramaic is written, in our manuscript and printed Bibles, exactly like Hebrew. There are the same twenty-two letters, all consonants, the same use of the four weak letters *'aleph, he, waw* and *yodh* for vowel sounds and the same system of vowel points and accents. The uniformity is complete, for they were the same Massoretes who put the finishing touches to the whole text of the Bible, the Aramaic parts as well as the Hebrew. Such treatment seems not to have done any violence to either language, for Hebrew and Aramaic are, as has been said, nearly related languages, which evolved along almost parallel lines: both sprang from the same Semitic stock and both learned the use of the alphabet from the Phoenicians. There is nothing surprising, then, in the fact that they were able during their history to exchange benefits in this way, Hebrew receiving the forms of the square alphabet from Aramaic, and Aramaic later profiting from the system of vocalization worked out for the whole Hebrew Bible.

THE NOUN

From the moment one first looks at Aramaic it is easy to find both similarities with and differences from Hebrew.

The grammatical structure of the noun is the same: two genders, three numbers (the dual rarely used), no declension properly so called, but the use of a construct state to denote possession. The principal difference is that Aramaic has no article like Hebrew's, but uses instead a "determinate state"[2]; that is, a special form of the noun called (wrongly) the *emphatic state*. So to the two "cases" of nominal inflexion in Hebrew—the absolute and construct states—Aramaic adds a third, the emphatic state, used for the determinate noun without a complement. Here as an example is the declension of a word common in Aramaic as in Hebrew, *melek*, king:

| | Masculine | | Feminine | |
	Singular	Plural	Singular	Plural
Absolute	melek	malkîn	malkâ'	malkân
Construct	melek	malkê	malkath	malkâth
Emphatic	malkâ'	malkayyâ'	malkᵉthâ'	malkâthâ'

The relationships with Hebrew are plain; so too are the differences, notably the plurals of the masculine in -*în* and of the feminine in -*ân*.

It is easy to recognize Aramaic forms such as, for example, the emphatic state in -*â'*, in several words handed down to us in the New Testament: abba—*'abbâ'* (Mark 14. 36, etc.); Golgotha —*Gulgoltâ'* (Matt. 27. 33); Talitha—*Talîthâ'* (Mark 5. 41); Tabitha—*Tabîthâ'* (Acts 9. 36, 40).

[2] This is doubtless also an article, but added to the noun as a suffix instead of being prefixed to it.

THE VERB

The conjugation of the verb in Aramaic works in much the same way as in Hebrew, but the actual verbal forms are sensibly different.

The three Aramaic forms correspond to the *simple, intensive* and *causative* of Hebrew: e.g. for the verb "to write" (Heb. *kâthabh*): *kethabh, kattibh* or *kattêbh* and *hakhtebh*; the last is sometimes replaced in certain verbs by another causative form with the preformative *shin: shakhtebh,* which shows Accadian influence.

In the other voices, the passive and reflexive, the differences are more noticeable. In many languages the reflexive form tends to replace the passive; in Greek, for example, we can see it in the relations between the passive and the middle, or the same tendency can be observed in the Romance languages' reflexive: *la maison se construit,* for example, for "the house is being built".

This process of substitution, which in Hebrew only affects the simple form (in which the reflexive *niqtal* has replaced the lost passive), goes much further in Aramaic and affects all forms, even those in which there is still a true passive, that is, the simple (*kethîbh*) and the first causative (*hokhtabh*).

So we get reflexive-passives for each of the four forms:

active	*kethabh*	reflexive	*hithkethebh*
	kattibh		*hithkattabh*
	hakhtebh		*hittakhtabh*
	shakhtebh		*hishtakhtabh*[3]

Which gives us, for the regular verb, the following table:

		active	passive	reflexive
simple		*kethabh*	*kethîbh*	*hithkethebh*
intensive		*kattibh*		*hithkattabh*
causative	}	*hakhtebh*	*hokhtabh*	*hittakhtabh*
		shakhtebh		*hishtakhtabh*

[3] For *hithshakhtabh,* by metathesis, to avoid *ts* or *tsh* (*ths* or *thsh*) which are impossible in Aramaic as in Hebrew.

Obviously such a table supposes some simplification, and would need notes on some details, such as vocalization in *ê* instead of *i* (*kattebh* for *kattibh*), the spelling with *'aleph* sometimes preferred to that with *he* (*'akhtebh* for *hakhtebh*), or the rarity of the causative in *shin* (attested for four verbs); what is given here is an idealized outline.

The conjugation of the tenses of the indicative also recalls that of the Hebrew verb:

Perfect		
	Singular	*Plural*
3rd person masculine	*keᵗhabh*	*keᵗhabhû*
— feminine	*kithᵉbhath*	*keᵗhabhâh*
2nd person masculine	*keᵗhabhtâ*	*keᵗhabhtun*
— feminine	*keᵗhabht*	⟨*keᵗhabhtin*⟩ [4]
1st person common	*kithᵉbheth*	*keᵗhabhnâ'*

Imperfect		
	Singular	*Plural*
3rd person masculine	*yikhtubh*	*yikhtᵉbhûn*
— feminine	*tikhtubh*	*yikhtᵉbhân*
2nd person masculine	*tihktubh*	*tihktᵉbhûn*
— feminine	⟨*tikhtᵉbhin*⟩ [4]	⟨*tikhtᵉbhân*⟩ [4]
1st person common	*'ekhtubh*	*nikhtubh*

Obviously there are in Aramaic also irregularities, caused by the presence in the root of weak letters or gutturals. Setting one against the other, the paradigms of Aramaic are not sensibly more difficult—nor simpler—than those of Hebrew.

THE USE OF THE TENSES

Here again the analogy is obvious: the perfect is the tense of completed action, and so of single or instantaneous action, and thus of action referred to as past. The imperfect is essentially

[4] Theoretical form not attested in Old Testament Aramaic.

the tense of incomplete action, and so of action repeated or carried on, and so finally of action referred to as present or future (even in the past, as sometimes the English imperfect: "he asked what she was doing the next day").

Aramaic has no consecutive use of the tenses. It has a jussive, and even some forms of the subjunctive. Altogether, it is, from the point of view of the syntax of the verb, simpler than Hebrew. To make up for this, it uses the participial construction more frequently, either to signify an action with no reference to its completion or incompletion (as for example in our simple present), or to strengthen or further define the meaning of a verb used in a finite form (narrative participle). So we frequently come across the formula *'anô we'âmerîn,* "they replied and said" (lit. "saying").

The absolute infinitive and its usage, so characteristic of Hebrew, are unknown in Aramaic. But its single infinitive, with or without a suffix, is used in a very flexible manner.

THE RELATIVE

The Aramaic relative, corresponding to the Hebrew *'asher,* is *dî,* a single, invariable form, as *'asher* is in Hebrew. But it is used in a much more varied and flexible way, introducing a system of subordination unknown in Hebrew.

Like *'asher,* it can be joined with a preposition to make compound conjunctions like *kedhî,* "as soon as"; *min-dî,* "since"; *'athar dî,* "in the place where"; *kol-qobhel dî,* "according as", "because"; etc.

But the particular, special use of the relative *dî* is in what may be called *imperfect relative clauses;* for example: "the Temple at (of) Jerusalem": *hêkhelâ' dî bîrushelem,* lit., "the temple which at Jerusalem" (1 Esdras 5. 14); "the vessels . . . of the house of God": *mâ'nayyâ' dhî-bêth-'elâhâ,* lit., "the vessels which (of) the house of God" (*ibid.*). It can be seen that in these cases the noun followed by the relative is in the emphatic state. The *dî* is gradually substituted for the classical construction with the construct state, and tends to become a preposition, like our "of" denoting possession. This process is the more interesting since it is also found in an ordinary Syriac idiom, generally with a pronoun suffix giving warning of the coming relative: "the vessels of it, of the house of God"; and again in Middle Hebrew with the word *shel* (compounded from the relative *she* and the particle *le*, and so meaning "which ⟨is⟩ of"), which is treated as a true preposition.

VOCABULARY

Such are some of the particular grammatical characteristics of Old Testament Aramaic. A few remarks are appended on the vocabulary.

Obviously there are some words which are common to Hebrew and Aramaic or are only distinguished by differences in vocalization: "father", *'ab*; "brother", *'aḥ*; "sign", *'âth* (Heb. *'ôth*); "all", *kol*; "head", *rê'sh* (Heb. *rô'sh*).

Others are more or less different in form[5]: "son", *bar*, (Heb. *ben*); "earth", *'ara'* (emphat. *'ar'â'*; Heb. *'ereç*); "three", *telâth* (Heb. *shâlôsh*).

Lastly there are some words, rare or poetical in classical Hebrew, which are normal, everyday words in Aramaic: "kill", *qetal*; "man", *'enâsh*; "receive", *qebal*; "come", *'athâ'*; "word", *millâh*.

In short, these are clearly two distinct languages. Their differences are such that at the time when Hebrew was the spoken language of Jerusalem, Aramaic was not understood by the man in the street and could be used for more or less confidential conversation (Isaias 36. 11-12).

Yet they are languages of the same family, and kept many features in common in their structure and in their vocabulary. The knowledge of the one makes the acquisition of the other a good deal easier, and we can say that one who has made some progress in Hebrew will learn the rudiments of Aramaic quickly and without too much trouble.

[5] It will be understood that these differences are generally explicable by the laws of phonetics, but we may be excused from going into such technicalities here.

CHAPTER VIII

ARAMAIC:
THE LITERATURE

A better acquaintance with Old Testament Aramaic will be possible if we set it in its linguistic context by giving a rapid sketch of the complicated world of Aramaic literature.

OLD ARAMAIC

Very few records of Old Aramaic have survived; we have nothing from before the tenth century, or possibly the ninth. This is not surprising, for the nomadic Arameans were doubtless ignorant of the art of writing and had only oral traditions.

What is more strange and more regrettable is that the Aramaic kingdoms of the tenth to eighth centuries have left us no literary work at all. Yet it is probable that there were writers, especially at Damascus, to judge from Ugarit some centuries earlier and Israel at about the same time. Their national literature would have been of the greatest interest for us, and we can only regret its disappearance.

All that has come down to us is a good dozen or so Old Aramaic inscriptions, one ostracon and one papyrus; precious remains, but insufficient for the study of the script and the language of that time. Almost all of this has been discovered recently, and we can hope that the luck of exploration and methodical digging will yet one day increase our knowledge of Old Aramaic.

ARAMAIC IN THE PERSIAN EMPIRE

After the disappearance of the Aramaic kingdoms, the language persisted and even spread beyond its ancient boundaries. So in the time of the Persian domination of the Near East we can speak of an "imperial Aramaic", a common language somewhat analogous to the Greek of the *koinê* some centuries later. Aramaic inscriptions have been found in Asia Minor, in Mesopotamia, in Persia, in Arabia, in the Caucasus, and even as far as Afghanistan and India. In Egypt there are not only inscriptions but more or less official records: letters of imperial functionaries, contracts, etc., and above all that collection of papyri and ostraca from Elephantine (Upper Egypt) which proves the existence, from the fifth century B.C., of a Jewish colony speaking Aramaic and reading Aramaic works (the *Tales of Ahikar*), and corresponding in that language with the authorities in Jerusalem and Samaria. In short, in the heterogeneous empire of the Achaemenids, imperial officials, military colonists, foreign merchants, everyone in that cosmopolitan world made himself generally understood in Aramaic.

NABATAEAN AND PALMYRENIAN

But Aramaic outlived the Persian empire. True, Greek followed the armies of Alexander, and easily made conquest of the educated classes, in the great commercial centres and the political capitals. But the people, especially in out of the way areas, remained loyal to their Semitic dialects. So, two centuries after the fall of the Achaemenids, Aramaic reappears, chiefly in inscriptions, in two little kingdoms on the edge of the Syrian desert, that of the Nabataeans, and that of Palmyra.

These were not strictly speaking Aramaic states. The Nabataeans were Arabs who organized themselves into a kingdom around Petra, in Idumaea, from the first century B.C. to the third century A.D. They spoke Arabic but wrote Aramaic, an Aramaic studded here and there both in vocabulary and grammar with Arabic words and forms. So they left at Petra and at numerous places on their distant wanderings inscriptions and graffiti written in a script with lengthened letters, and often accompanied by a Greek translation. Recent discoveries in the desert of Judah have even brought to light Nabataean records on papyrus, but only one has so far been published.

At about the same time the city of Palmyra came into prominence as an important commercial centre. The city developed considerably under the protection or the authority of the Roman Empire, until it saw, under Queen Zenobia, an extraordinary political venture which led to its ruin in A.D. 273. From 44 B.C. to the date of the city's destruction, there stretches a series of votive or funerary inscriptions, in Aramaic, in Greek or in both. The Aramaic, which was the spoken language of Palmyra, is less influenced by Arabic than that of the Nabataeans; but it shows evidence instead of appreciable influence from the east. Its restrained and elegant script recalls that of certain texts from the desert of Judah.

PALESTINIAN ARAMAIC

It was, however, in Palestine that Aramaic took root most deeply and had the most lasting influence, for it succeeded in supplanting Hebrew as the popular tongue and existed alongside of it as a literary language even into the Jewish circles of the west in the Middle Ages.

It began to establish itself, perhaps, in Samaria, a land more cosmopolitan and open to foreign influences than Judaea. Several important memorials of early Aramaic were produced there: an *Aramaic targum of the Pentateuch*,[1] possibly of great antiquity; a *commentary on the Pentateuch*, only partially preserved and attributed to the poet Marqâ (fourth century); and the *Samaritan liturgy*, built up over the centuries, from the

---

[1] Sometimes called the "Samaritan Pentateuch", but this name is kept rather for the Samaritan edition of the Hebrew Pentateuch written in Samaritan characters. Both texts were published for the first time in the Paris polyglot of 1645. The Pentateuch was the only book admitted as sacred by the Samaritans.

5—S.L.

pre-Christian era to the Middle Ages, and still used in our own days.

It was bound, however, to be considerably less successful among orthodox Jewry.

We have seen that two fairly considerable fragments of Aramaic have been included in the Bible. The older seems to be that of the book of Esdras (4. 8—6. 18 and 7. 12-26). It reproduces documents assigned, the one lot to the fifth century (the beginning of the reign of Artaxerxes I, 465-424), the other probably to the beginning of the fourth (the seventh year of the reign of Artaxerxes II, 405-359). These constitute valuable evidence of Aramaic in Palestine at an early period. It is true that there are indications which have led scholars to think that they have been at least worked over by a late reviser, perhaps by the Chronicler himself. But in spite of this, comparison with the principal documents from Elephantine on the one hand, and with the text of Daniel on the other, show that they are closer to the Elephantine documents than to the book of Daniel. They have not been distorted by the reviser and we can appeal to them in reconstituting the evolution of the language.

As for the fragment of Daniel (2. 4—7. 28), this is a narrative passage the presence of which between passages of Hebrew remains unexplained. Whatever the explanation, if the final edition of the book is dated to the first half of the second century B.C., the Aramaic chapters can be considered to be a little earlier.

Recent discoveries have appreciably increased our knowledge of Aramaic literature in Palestine in the last centuries B.C. In particular fragments have been discovered of several manuscripts of the *book of Enoch*, remains of a *Testament of Levi*, which is perhaps a little later, a *midrash on Genesis* and a number of unidentified pieces.

In the first century A.D. Aramaic was the language generally spoken in Palestine. It was therefore the mother tongue of Jesus, that in which the Gospel was first proclaimed. One would give a great deal to find one document dating certainly from that time, particularly for the Aramaic sources from which some pages of our canonical Gospels were written. At least we can hope that more light will be shed on the background to the New Testament as the documents from the desert of Judah are published, studied and dated.

Certainly the use of the targum was established in the first century. That is to say, it was necessary to translate into Aramaic, for the benefit of the great majority of the listeners, the Bible texts read in Hebrew in the synagogues. If it was at first only a matter of oral interpretation, of paraphrases more or less improvised, it was soon necessary, for convenience' sake, to write down these translations and make collections of them. Some passages of the midrash on Genesis mentioned above probably belong to this kind of writing, and would therefore represent the oldest known fragments of the Targum. Next to them we must mention the *Palestinian Targum of the Pentateuch*, of which only portions have survived, either discovered in the Cairo Geniza,[2] or identified in the more recent work, which has been somewhat adapted, called the *Jerusalem Targum*. But these Palestinian targums were replaced, possibly about the sixth century, by the *Targum Onkelos*, which came out of the schools of Babylonia but was recognized as official by the whole of Jewry. Another targum of the Pentateuch, called the *Targum of Pseudo-Jonathan*, is derived from both the Palestinian targum and that of Onkelos.

The targum of the prophets ("former" and "latter", that is the historical books and the prophets) is generally attributed to Jonathan ben Uzziel, a disciple of Hillel in the first century A.D. But though it does certainly include passages from older targums it probably comes from Babylonia and also depends upon the Targum Onkelos.

As for the Talmud, we have already remarked (p. 52) that though the *Mishnah* was still written in Hebrew, its later commentary, the *Gemara*, is mostly in Aramaic. The Jerusalem

---

[2] A *geniza* is a place where the Jews deposited sacred books no longer fit for use in the synagogue; the Geniza of Old Cairo, explored in and after 1890, contained a vast quantity of documents accumulated over the centuries.

Talmud, made by the Jews of Galilee, at Sephoris or Tiberias, between the third and fifth centuries, is the clearest proof of a distinct Palestinian Aramaic dialect. As much could be said of the Hebrew texts of the *Midrashim* (pp. 52–3) which include scattered fragments of Aramaic, evidence of the language spoken in Galilee in the first centuries of our era.

But gradually, in its turn, Aramaic ceased to be a spoken language. Then, it was up against Hebrew, on the one hand, with its immense prestige among the Jews, and the living languages of the west and Arabic, on the other. It lost some of its importance, without ever altogether ceasing to be used, either in the liturgy or in the schools.

So one of the greatest books of Judaism was produced in Aramaic even in the Middle Ages, the *Zohar* (Splendour), an allegorical and mystical commentary on the Pentateuch, together with treatises different in kind but similar in spirit. The compilation must have been begun about the tenth century, but it was not finished or published, by Moses ben Shem-Tob de Leon, until about 1300.

CHRISTIAN ARAMAIC

Alongside of this abundant Jewish literature the by no means negligible remains of Christian writings must not be forgotten. The most important of them is a lectionary which gives us, in particular, pericopes (sections, passages selected for reading) from the Gospels translated into Palestinian Aramaic. There are also some hymns, homilies and hagiographic legends, as well as some inscriptions and at least one papyrus document. It is difficult to place all this exactly in time or geographically; yet it does testify to the persistence in Palestine, and perhaps further afield, for a long period, of groups of Aramaic-speaking Christians.

EASTERN ARAMAIC

This other dialect of later Aramaic is known to us chiefly by two groups of sources, the Babylonian Talmud and the Mandean writings.

The Babylonian Talmud is perceptibly later than that of Jerusalem; like it, the order of the treatises of the mishnah which are being commented upon is followed, but it is fuller, richer and more varied. It is this one which is quoted as "the Talmud".

The Mandeans are a more or less gnostic sect, curiously blending Jewish elements with Christian traditions; they have lived from time immemorial in Lower Mesopotamia. The various compilations that make up the literature of the sect—*Ginzâ rabbâ*, "The Great Treasure"; *Sidrâ d'Yahyâ*, "The Book of John" (the Baptist); *Qolastâ*, "Selections"—to which must be added many unpublished writings, magical formulae, etc., show us a language related to that of the Talmud, but which has evolved in this one locality and been quite free from any Hebrew influence. The rigorously separatist and conservative character of the sect has made it possible for them to preserve more authentic eastern elements than are found in the writings of the Jews.

SYRIAC

We should give a very incomplete idea of eastern Aramaic literature did we not add a few words on Syriac. Syriac is simply an eastern branch of Aramaic established in Upper Mesopotamia and Syria which became, around Edessa, a Christian language. Written in a fine cursive script, made more flexible by contact with Greek civilization, and developed specially for theological purposes, Syriac was capable of an abundant production of books from the second to the seventeenth century.

We must content ourselves here with mentioning only a few of these books. In the second century we have translations of the Gospels; the famous *Diatessaron* of Tatian, of which the Syriac text has unfortunately been lost; a translation of the Bible (the "Peshitta") made from the Hebrew but influenced by the Septuagint. From a little later we may mention, apart from liturgical texts, the works of the famous philosopher

Bardesanes (second to third century), of the bishop Aphraates (third to fourth century), and lastly, and especially, the great St Ephrem (300–373), deacon of Edessa, religious poet and commentator on the Bible.

From the fifth century onwards painful divisions in the Syriac community were caused by theological quarrels. First a Nestorian Church split from the Catholic core and moved towards the east, around the town of Nisibis. A century later the Bishop of Edessa, James of Tella, surnamed Baradai, organized a dissident hierarchy in his Church professing the Monophysite heresy. Political divisions exacerbated these doctrinal differences: the easterns, the Nestorians, belonged to the Persian empire; the westerns, the Monophysites, to the Roman. So they developed two dialects, with their own peculiarities of script, pronunciation, and grammar.

Each of these Churches showed active signs of life in a vast literary output. Names such as those of Narses (fifth–sixth century) and Babai (sixth–seventh century) among the Nestorians, and John of Ephesus (sixth century), James of Edessa (seventh–eighth century), and even James bar Salibi (twelfth century) and the bishop Barhebreus (died in 1286), among the Monophysites, are proof of that vitality.

But gradually, from the eighth century onwards, Arabic took the place of Syriac, which then fell into disuse both as a spoken and as a literary language.

Nowadays it is only spoken by rare isolated groups. Eastern Syriac is spoken by the Nestorian and Uniate Chaldaean inhabitants of some villages of Iraq, especially to the north of Mosul, and a few recent communities of "refugees" in Syria and in Baghdad. Western Syriac is spoken in three villages in Syria to the north of Damascus, the best known being Ma'loula, a Christian village; in Iraq, to the south-east of Mosul, among the Catholics and Monophysites; and in north-west Syria among the Monophysites who emigrated there from Turkey during the First World War.

Syriac has, however, chiefly survived as a liturgical language, in the Chaldaean rite of the Nestorian and Catholic Chaldaean

Churches, in the Syrian rite of the Monophysite and Uniate Syrian Churches and in the Maronite rite, which is solely Catholic and is mostly represented in the Lebanon. Lastly, the Chaldaean rite has also spread to Malabar among the Indian population.

PART II

GREEK

by Pierre Poulain

CHAPTER IX

THE LANGUAGE OF THE MEDITERRANEAN WORLD

It was the providential good fortune of Christianity to have been able to express the Word of God in a language understood by the whole of the then civilized world, just as it was the good fortune of the first Christian missionaries to have been able to travel freely throughout a world where except for local disturbances the *pax Romana* ruled, the Roman peace. "One of the greatest of mystical mysteries—I must be allowed to join these two words—is the necessity of Rome in the temporal purpose of God. In order that the Christian world might assume that temporal form which it was to receive and keep, the arch and empire, the *vallum* and *testudo*, had to exist." These pages [1] should be read, in which Péguy extols the part of the Roman legions in the unification of the Mediterranean world, which was to become the Christian world. But history demands that their importance be regarded as somewhat less than he suggests. The Mediterranean world did not wait for the Roman legions before making a kind of cultural commonwealth. When in the second century the two worlds met, it was Greece, not Rome, which won the victory in the cultural sphere: *Graecia capta ferum victorem cepit*—"conquered Greece took captive her barbaric captor", as Horace says [2]—since for more than a century Greece had been the teacher of the world. And

---

[1] Charles Péguy, *Basic Verities*; translations by Ann and Julian Green (London, Kegan Paul, 1943), pp. 158 ff; New York, Pantheon.
[2] *Epist.*, II, i, 156.

the chief architect of this intellectual conquest, in which he himself saw a divine mission, was Alexander the Great, as Plutarch says:

> But, as he believed that he came as a heaven-sent governor to all, and as a mediator for the whole world, those whom he could not persuade to unite with him, he conquered by force of arms, and he brought together into one body all men everywhere, uniting and mixing in one great loving-cup, as it were, men's lives, their characters, their marriages, their very habits of life. He bade them all consider as their fatherland the whole inhabited earth, as their stronghold and protection his camp, as akin to them all good men, and as foreigners only the wicked; they should not distinguish between Grecian and foreigner by Grecian cloak and targe, or scimitar and jacket: but the distinguishing mark of the Grecian should be seen in virtue, and that of the foreigner in iniquity.[3]

THE SPREAD OF THE KOINÊ

The *koinê* was the common tongue spoken and written after the conquests of Alexander throughout the Hellenistic world. Apart from numerous borrowings from Ionian it was basically Attic Greek, which means we must push back its origins to the time when the pre-eminence of Athens was established. After the Persian wars, and particularly after the victory of Salamis in 480, Athens increased her hold on the Aegean islands and the south coast of Italy. It is true that her maritime empire was very short-lived, even if we take into account the brief revival which followed the Peloponnesian War. But if Athens was not for long the most powerful city militarily, she always kept up relations with many of the Greek cities through her commercial undertakings, so that her soldiers, her administrators and especially her merchants, spread everywhere the language they spoke.

But it was above all the cultural prestige of Athens which assured the triumph of Attic as the language of educated people. As Florence was to impose its literary language on all the

[3] Plutarch, *On the Fortune of Alexander*; Moralia, 329 C (vol. IV of Loeb Classical Library edn, trans. F. C. Babbitt, 1936).

Italian courts, as in the eighteenth century French was to be spoken at the courts of Frederick II and of Catherine the Great, so Athens imposed the language of her writers on most of the tyrants of the Greek world. The Macedonian court in particular seems to have adopted the Attic dialect from the fifth century on. Plato could put this claim in the mouth of the Stranger of the *Laws*: "Each of us regards it (*sc.* Athens) as a second motherland, next after his own country." [4]

But already Thucydides, if the attribution of the Palatine Anthology is to be believed, had called Athens the "Hellas of Hellas". [5] And the *Panegyricus* of Isocrates was not only the expression of national pride; it was really to Athens that men came from all over the civilized world to be educated in philosophy and rhetoric.

When he conquered Egypt, and then Asia as far as the Indus, Alexander took into these regions the culture he had received from his master Aristotle. The cities founded by him and his successors—Alexandria, Pergamon, Antioch—were to become the great centres of Hellenistic civilization. The Roman world itself could not escape the seductiveness of Hellenism. To each of the military victories of Rome there corresponded a sort of inverse victory of Hellenism, a cultural victory. The more the triumphal march of her legions and the skilful diplomacy of her senate extended her dominion over Campania, South Italy, Greece, Asia and Egypt, the more Rome was exposed to Greek influence. So much so that when the Empire had achieved the unity of the Mediterranean world it became a bilingual society, in which whoever wanted to play a part of any importance took care to acquire some Greek education, *paideia*.

The flowering of Latin literature in the age of Cicero and Augustus did nothing to lessen the hold which Hellenism had on Roman culture from the second century B.C. onwards. At school, Roman children learned Greek before they learned Latin, and studied alongside one another Cicero and Demosthenes,

---

[4] Plato, *Laws*, 642 B; trans. R. G. Bury (Loeb Classical Library, 1926).
[5] *Anth. Pal.*, VII, 45; in vol. II of *The Greek Anthology*, trans. W. R. Paton (Loeb Classical Library, 1919).

Homer and Virgil; the Roman aristocracy crowded to hear the Greek orators; it was in Greek that Marcus Aurelius wrote his private journal in the rare intervals of leisure his service of the state allowed him. It was not before the middle of the third century that the Church of Rome adopted Latin in its liturgy, probably under the influence of the Church in north Africa. It is only at the end of the fourth that there is a noticeable decline in Greek culture in the west. St Augustine, who had learned Greek—not without tears, he admits in the *Confessions*—forgot it, and had to make an effort about the year 400 to relearn it, in order to read in the original the New Testament and the writings of the eastern Fathers.

In the eastern half of the Empire, except for the necessary dealings with the imperial government, Latin was not used. "The Greek world never made the slightest effort to assimilate the culture of Rome, and the Christian east showed the same proud indifference to the Latin language as to the learned men who taught in that language in Gaul, in Africa and in Spain."[6] It was only on the borders of the Empire, where Greek culture had never completely taken root, that the Church, desirous of reaching the mass of the people, who remained faithful to their "barbaric" tongues, brought into being a religious literature, around translations of the Bible, in Coptic and Syriac, whose influence remained purely local.

So the linguistic unity of the Mediterranean world, begun even before Alexander's conquests, was to last more than six centuries, making easy the spread first of the message of Israel and then of the Gospel of Christ.

CHARACTERISTICS OF THE KOINÊ: "BIBLICAL" GREEK

When Alexander's conquests opened the barbarian world to the Greek language, it already had behind it more than a thousand years of history. Our ideas of this history were

[6] G. Bardy, *La question des langues dans l'Eglise ancienne*, p. 155 (Paris, Beauchesne, 1948).

profoundly changed in 1953 when Michael Ventris and John Chadwick published the first results of a brilliant feat of deciphering. The Cretan "Linear B" script, which up till then had remained a mystery, was shown to represent, by a syllabary of sorts which preceded the use of the Phoenician alphabet, a very archaic Greek dialect which has been called "old Achaean" or "Mycenean" and which was spoken in Crete and the Peloponnese between 1500 and 1200 B.C. Only a number of graven tablets, with no literary document, survive from that period, but this decipherment confirms what was already conjectured: the Homeric poems do not mark the beginnings but surely the culmination of a literature the minor works of which have been lost. It is well known how great was the influence on Greek poetry, throughout its history, of Homer's work; read and learned by heart in the schools, commented on by the learned, it was the bible of the Greeks.

Literature in prose began much later with the work of Herodotus in the middle of the fifth century, and in Attic with Thucydides at the end of that century. To begin with this prose was somewhat crude and often obscure, for the difficulty of expressing closely-knit thought produced some awkwardness of phraseology. But in the hands of the sophists and orators, who needed it to possess clarity and a supple persuasiveness once eloquence had become of great practical importance, it became simpler and more flexible.

There is no need to enter here on a long study of the Greek language; it would be otiose for those who know the language and without interest for those who do not. All that is necessary is to mark some of the characteristics which make it such a superb instrument for the expression of the finest shades of meaning—not to mention that quality referred to by Swinburne as "the clear music of the flutes of Greece".

More archaic than Latin, Greek preserved more clearly certain Indo-European characteristics, the most important of which are:

1. The existence alongside one another of two distinct forms of the verb, inaccurately called the "present" and the "aorist"

(Gk., "indeterminate"), allows the expression (a) by the aorist, of the simple achievement of action, its instantaneous completion: ἀπέθανε, "he died"; ἐχάρη, "he rejoiced"; or (b) by the present or imperfect, the continuous, inchoative, or incomplete character of an action: ἀπέθνῃσκε, "he was dying"; ἐδίδου, "he offered", rather than "he was giving". In the other moods this distinction of *Aktionsart*, the kind of action, allows the difference to be made, for example, between μὴ φοβεῖσθε, "calm yourselves, stop being afraid", and μὴ φοβήθητε, "do not be afraid", "keep calm". These shades of meaning, which are always there right down to modern Greek, often demand very great care and precision in translation. Again, still on the subject of "tenses", Greek preserved some ancient "perfects" which are intransitive and express a state: πέποιθα, "I am confident, I trust"; ἕστηκα, "I am standing up, I stand"; οἶδα, "I know". In a general way the classical language used the perfect to denote not so much finished action as the result which follows from an action.

2. The preservation of the optative, an indistinct future mood, of what is simply possible or desired, allows very subtle distinctions to be drawn—which English can also draw, but often in ways less simple or logical. "If he should come", for example, is distinguished from "if he comes", and "would that he would come" from "let him come". Together with the optative we may consider the existence of a modal particle ἄν, the use of which, prescribed in Attic by fairly precise rules, causes great trouble to beginners in Greek. It allows meanings to be very finely distinguished. If it be joined to an optative it gives to an affirmation or a command a more mild or polite aspect; this polite optative was regarded as a mark of courtesy: it corresponds to our "I might say" or "would you mind?"

3. Lastly, the very numerous prepositions remained in Greek close to their adverbial origins. They were originally formed to express all space relations of movement and situation, and became associated with nouns so as to make more precise the relationships already imperfectly expressed by the cases. Above all, joined to verbal forms they produced the great number of compound and even doubly compound verbs, so as to translate

into words in a synthetic and extremely precise way all the real or imaginary directions and relations of action, and what we may call the mental gestures in our thought: so συνδιασῶσαι τὴν χώραν means exactly "to ensure, by one's own participation, the safety of the country".

The Greek spoken in the Hellenistic world was at once the same and yet very different. Its spread brought with it consequences which changed it considerably. To begin with the Attic we know from the great classical works is a literary language, an artistic prose. The carefully balanced periods of Isocrates reveal to us the preparation and effort that go into their writing. The spontaneity of Demosthenes' speeches, which give the impression of having been improvised to suit the reactions of his audience, is a prepared spontaneity, if one may put it so, the result of study and long experience of that audience. The flowing prose of Plato's dialogues, which seems to proceed with the meandering gait of ordinary conversation, is yet carefully and infinitely varied. At times it is easy, relaxed, almost incorrect; it tramps along heavily, slowed down by the denseness of the supposed speaker. At times, as in the *Apology* or some pages of the *Phaedo*, or the *Phaedrus* or the *Republic*, it lifts itself to sublimity. As opposed to this, the Greek we read in the Scriptures is a spoken, popular language, in which considerations of style are rarely apparent. The Greek translation of the Old Testament and the writings of the New Testament can give us some idea of the changes Greek passed through, much more than the works of Menander or Polybius, who remained strongly influenced by the classical language despite their innovations.

Not to mention purely morphological changes, the following points at least ought to be noticed:

1. If the translators of the Old Testament made many mistakes in their use of the tenses, because of the special difficulty of rendering the Hebrew "tenses", the New Testament authors observed the essential distinction, so deeply rooted in the language, between the present and the aorist. The *koinê* made no innovation here. As for the perfect, a tendency can be seen developing—already perceptible in Demosthenes—to use it not

6—S.L.

to express the present state which is the result of past action, but simply for the emphatic statement of the action done, so that it becomes an emphatic past tense whose expressive value should not be over-estimated.[7]

2. The optative tends to disappear, for its nice distinctions of meaning demand a real feeling for the language. Its use was a sign of education, so it is not surprising that Luke, the most educated of the evangelists, provides us with the most examples. The polite optative with ἄν practically disappeared and the optative in dependent clauses, the "oblique" optative, is only to be met in Luke. In fact, almost the only optative to survive is the optative of wishing, and this moreover practically reduced to a fixed formula, familiar in Paul: μὴ γένοιτο, *God forbid!*

3. In accordance with the general tendency of Indo-European languages to prefer analytical constructions prepositions were used more and more. But their meanings became less precise, so that we often find one used for another. Compound verbs were often hardly different in meaning from their simple forms, and this very weakening led to the multiplication of compound forms. For similar reasons compound prepositions were formed, such as ἀπέναντι and κατέναντι, analogous to our *into* and *round about*; and, influenced by Hebrew, in prepositional phrases compounded with πρόσωπον, *in front of.*

The second point is that the *koinê* was generally spoken by people who were bilingual. Now it is inevitable, except with very well educated people, that the language which is learned should be adulterated by the mother tongue. This rather trite observation may allow us to attack the problem of the Semitisms in Biblical Greek peaceably and calmly, though it has been the cause of very lively controversy. To someone passing from the reading of the classical writers to the Bible the Greek of the latter presents an appearance so different that there is a temptation to regard it as a special, isolated language with its own laws; one will point out with a shudder its incorrectness, while another will admire the unexpected effects of inspiration.

[7] The perfect is especially frequent in the Johannine works; it is a mark of solemnity.

We can indeed with good right speak of a language of the Holy Ghost. For in the Bible it is manifest to our eyes how the Divine Spirit at work in revelation always takes the language of the particular people chosen to be the recipient and makes of it a characteristic religious variety by transforming existing linguistic elements and existing conceptions into a shape peculiarly appropriate to that Spirit. This process is shown most clearly by the Greek of the New Testament.[8]

Without going as far as that, many scholars at the end of the last century followed J. Viteau in inclining towards a judaizing Greek as a dialect peculiar to the Jews of the Diaspora. But the philological study of the numberless papyri discovered in the sands of Egypt throughout the nineteenth century opened the problem afresh. After the studies of Deissmann and Thumb the isolated position of "Biblical Greek" became mythical. The list of words up till then considered purely Biblical was reduced as they were found in the published papyri. And many of the syntactical peculiarities which had been attributed to the influence of the Semitic languages appeared rather to be vulgarisms or errors due to ignorance of the language, examples of which were furnished by the papyri.

The arguments and opinions of Deissmann and Thumb have been generally accepted by Hellenists but have been the objects of continual protest from Hebrew and Aramaic scholars. They regard it as insufficient that a word or mode of expression should be found here and there in a papyrus to entitle one to deny the influence of Semitic precisely where one is dealing with writers accustomed to reading the Bible or whose native tongue was Aramaic. Besides, the affirmation of such influence is justified by the coincidence with Semitic usage of the frequency of certain fixed phrases or expressions or of certain unclassical uses. There are expressions, some of which have even passed into English through the translations, such as those with an adjectival genitive, as οἱ υἱοὶ τοῦ φωτός, *sons of light*, or an odd use of a

---

[8] R. Rothe, *Zur Dogmatik* (Gotha, 1853), p. 238, quoted by A. Deissmann, *The Philology of the Greek Bible*, trans. by L. R. M. Strachan from the author's MS (London, 1908), p. 42.

preposition, as ὁμολογέω ἐν, *to acknowledge* (*someone*), which are not Greek but literal translations of Hebrew or Aramaic idioms.

Some recent studies have supported those who maintain that there has been Semitic influence. Certain peculiarities in the Biblical text which had been classed as Semitisms and which are also found in the papyri have been shown to be explicable in the latter by analogous forms of Egyptian syntax and cannot therefore be claimed as belonging to Hellenistic Greek. One important conclusion has gradually emerged from all these discussions among the specialists: the changes which bilingual speakers bring about in a language concern not so much vocabulary and syntax as the meanings of words and style. The translators of the Hebrew Bible and those who in their original works continued its message used, with rare exceptions, Greek words; but they often gave them a quite new connotation. As for the authors of the New Testament, their vocabulary like their modes of thought, depends strictly on the Biblical tradition. It is thus in this sense above all that we can speak of "Biblical Greek".

CHAPTER X

THE GREEK TRANSLATION OF THE OLD TESTAMENT

"There will be an altar set up to the Lord for all Egypt to see . . . thus the Lord will reveal himself to Egypt" (Isaias 19. 19 and 21). This spiritual conquest of Egypt, in which the prophet saw one of the elements of the eschatological triumph of Israel, was to be made a reality by the importance of Alexandrian Judaism and then of the Christian school of Alexandria in the spread of Jewish and Christian thought over the pagan world. The Babylonian exile was the tragic beginning of a movement of expansion of the Jews which never ceased in all the centuries to come. Those who returned from Babylon after the edict of Cyrus left behind in Mesopotamia an important Jewish colony which was to play a great part in the history of the Roman Empire and of the Middle Ages. But the essential point is that there were a great many Jewish communities in the Hellenistic world, and first in Egypt.

That Hellenism to which the Palestinian Jews offered armed and finally successful resistance under the Machabees never met with the same violent opposition in Egypt. When Alexander founded the city of Alexandria in 332 he looked with a favourable eye on Jewish colonists: "Having found among them brave and loyal allies he granted that they might settle in a quarter of the new city with legal rights equal to those of the Greeks." [1] This Jewish colony remained flourishing under the rule of his successors, the Ptolemies, whose liberal policies may be contrasted with those of the Seleucids, and its prosperity drew to it a large

[1] Josephus, *Bell. Jud.*, II, 18, 7.

number of Palestinian Jews. According to Philo,[2] the Jews in
Alexandria in the first century A.D. made up two fifths of the
total population, and the proportion of Jews in the whole
Hellenistic world, on which Rome imposed political unity during
the second and third centuries, has been put as high as one in
ten—or even perhaps one in five in the eastern half of the
Empire. So Philo could call Jerusalem "the mother city not of a
single country but of most of the world, because of the colonies
she has sent out in swarms in past ages". When the author of the
Acts of the Apostles lists those who have come to Jerusalem
from all over the world for the Pentecost after the resurrection
of our Lord, he gives us some idea, an incomplete idea no
doubt, of the extent of the dispersion of the Jews at the beginning of the Christian era.

It was in the Jewish community of Alexandria that the
revelation of the Old Testament put on the Greek dress in
which, by means of first Jewish and then Christian missionaries,
it was to conquer the Mediterranean world.

> That the sanctity of our legislation has been a source of wonder
> not only to the Jews but also to all other nations, is clear both
> from the facts already mentioned and those which I proceed to
> state . . . some people, thinking it a shame that the laws should
> be found in one half only of the human race, the barbarians, and
> denied altogether to the Greeks, took steps to have them trans-
> lated. In view of the importance and public utility of the task, it
> was referred not to private persons or magistrates, who were very
> numerous, but to kings, and amongst them to the king of highest
> repute, Ptolemy, surnamed Philadelphus. . . .[3]

That is how Philo of Alexandria introduces his account of the
making of the Septuagint. Before him the story had been told
at length in the Letter of Pseudo-Aristeas,[4] written probably
around the year 100 B.C.

[2] *In Flaccum*, 6, 8; see also W. W. Tarn, *Hellenistic Civilization* (London,
1930), pp. 188 ff; 3rd edn, 1952, New York, St Martin's Press.
[3] Philo, *De Vita Mosis*, II, 25–8 (translated by F. H. Colson, Loeb
Classical Library, 1935; vol. VI, p. 461).
[4] See R. H. Pfeiffer, *Introduction to the Old Testament*, 5th edn (New
York, Harper, 1941), p. 104 f., and Bibliography, p. 881.

HISTORY AND CONTENT OF THE SEPTUAGINT

The letter pretends to have been written by Aristeas, a pagan official of the king Ptolemy II Philadelphus (285–247), the second successor of Alexander on the throne of Egypt. Aristeas is supposedly telling his brother Philocrates how he had been concerned in the business of the translation of the Law of Moses. Demetrius of Phalerum, the head of the Library of Alexandria, wished to add a translation of the Jewish law to its two hundred thousand volumes, and at his request the king wrote to the High Priest in Jerusalem, Eleazar. He had, he said, signed a decree freeing some hundred thousand Jews enslaved by his father Ptolemy I. This act of liberality was intended to bear witness to his piety and his gratitude to the supreme God to whom he owed the peace and prosperity of his kingdom. He then asked the High Priest to send to Alexandria seventy-two elders, six from each tribe, chosen for their wisdom and for their perfect acquaintance both with Hebrew and Greek. The letter, along with costly gifts, was taken to Jerusalem by an embassy including our Aristeas, and the visit gave them an opportunity to admire the Holy City, the Temple, the splendour of the sacrifices, the beauty of Palestine and the richness of the soil. They also took the chance of asking about the meaning of certain Jewish laws condemning idolatry and uncleanness. The seventy-two translators were then welcomed to Alexandria, where the king gave them a magnificent reception and a banquet lasting seven whole days. Each was then questioned in turn— ten a day to begin with and eleven on each of the last two days —and each showed himself to be outstandingly learned: ethics, philosophy, art of government—reading their replies is like reading one of those "manuals of the perfect prince" of which Isocrates' exhortation to Nicocles is the first example; but at least the commonplaces are here enlivened by constant reference to the God of Israel. At last, gathered together in the calm seclusion of the island of Pharos the seventy-two translators set to work. Their work, completed in seventy-two days, was read before the Jewish colony and found perfect, and a curse was invoked against whoever should alter the text.

This account was generally admitted as correct down to the Renaissance, though certain historical improbabilities sufficiently show its legendary character. It even received some embellishments, which were pruned away by the sharp critical sense of St Jerome. The seventy-two scribes, it was said, were shut up each in his own cell to translate the whole work and when their independent versions were compared they were found to be miraculously identical, word for word.

We can learn very little from Pseudo-Aristeas about the true origins of the Septuagint. The bias it reveals is considerably later than its supposed date; it is really a sign of the desire of the Alexandrian Jews to gain the sympathy of their pagan fellow-citizens and to attract proselytes to their faith by getting rid of the wall of misunderstanding which cut them off. But the origin of the Greek translation of the Old Testament is most probably rather to be sought in the needs within the synagogue of Alexandria. The Hebrew text of the Law had quickly become unintelligible to the Jewish population resident in Egypt, and it had become necessary to replace it for the purposes of the liturgy by a translation into the vulgar tongue.

The first texts translated were the five books which make up the Law, the Pentateuch, and it is only of this piece of translation that the letter of Pseudo-Aristeas speaks. It was doubtless made, as the letter says, in the first half of the third century, but by Alexandrian, not Palestinian, Jews. The versions of the Prophets and the other books were then added at times and in conditions we cannot now determine. Producing his work at the end of the second century the translator of Ecclesiasticus mentions in his prologue the tripartite division of the Hebrew Bible, which therefore existed in that form at the date when he was writing, but we cannot be sure that it contained all the books we now find in it, nor, what is most important, that all had been at that time translated into Greek.

In fact, the Septuagint remained for a long time an unclosed collection, to which more could be added. Besides the translations

of books of the Hebrew Bible, the manuscripts contain a
certain number of writings which, whether originally written
in Greek or translated from the Hebrew, were not admitted
into the canon of inspired Scriptures by the Jews of Palestine.
These books, which are called "deutero-canonical" because
their canonicity was the object of discussion during the patristic
period, were none the less reverently used by the Hellenistic
Jews, who recognized in them a development of revelation. It
is worth noting that at the present time the American Jewish
university, Dropsie College, has undertaken to re-edit them,
expressly regretting that the Jewish tradition allowed them to
be forgotten and rejoicing that the Christian tradition preserved
them.

ITS PHILOLOGICAL AND THEOLOGICAL IMPORTANCE

The "atticist" reaction of the first century of the Empire
encouraged a return to the norms of the Attic language as it
was written in the golden age of the fifth and fourth centuries
B.C. The result of this reaction was the disappearance of much
of the work of the Hellenistic period, of which only fragments
have been preserved. At the same time the strictness of the
Synagogue condemned to oblivion almost all the Jewish literature in Greek of the last two centuries before Christ. Preserved
by the Church, the Greek Bible has thus an exceptional interest
for linguistic scholars: it is one of the best sources for our
knowledge of the koinê. From the point of view of their literary
value the writings it contains offer a very wide range. At one
end of the scale we find the almost barbaric language of the
translators of the Pentateuch and the Prophets, men of very
little education above all desirous of providing their fellow-
worshippers with an understandable version of the Scriptures.
At the other end there are the late works, written directly in
Greek by educated Jews who wanted to reach their pagan contemporaries so that they should understand and perhaps even
accept and share their faith. The four books of Machabees, for
example, are very different from one another. While the first

seems to follow closely in its style a lost Hebrew original, the second, a summary of a history written in Greek by a man called Jason of Cyrene, uses a much richer vocabulary and a deliberately emphatic style: passages such as that describing the arrival of Heliodorus in Jerusalem (ch. 3) or that telling of the martyrdom of Eleazar and his seven brothers (chs. 6 and 7) are good examples of that pathos which was so loved in Alexandria in the second century B.C. The fourth book on the other hand is a complete philosophical treatise after the manner of the Stoics' "diatribes". In it the panegyric of the martyrs, written in accordance with the best rhetorical rules, is presented so as to show that courage can master the passions when upheld by piety and reason.

The Septuagint is still more important to the theologian. For a long time it was studied mainly in order to use the Greek to correct the Hebrew text, the manuscripts of which are all, with the exception of those recently discovered near the Dead Sea, several centuries later than the Greek version. It is true that this use is still possible and fruitful, for the translator followed his original closely and some slight variations lead one to suppose that he had a text different from and better than that we have now, while sometimes, on the other hand, there are divergences explicable only by his incompetence where the Hebrew text is to be preferred. But a deeper study often shows that it is less a matter of different readings or unconscious misinterpretation than of a really independent interpretation which can go so far as to modify the substance of the thought of a passage or even of a whole book.

Some books present to us an extremely literal version, as, for example, the Pentateuch; but it is also so in the case of a book translated later, Ecclesiastes, which thus poses a critical problem of its own. Not only has the translator followed the order of the words in the Hebrew very exactly, as if in an inter-linear version, but he carries his exactitude so far as to use expressions the artificial nature of which is strikingly obvious: the particle *eth*, which is prefixed to a definite object in Hebrew, is regularly rendered by σύν (with) without any change in the accusative which follows; *gam* or *megam* (also, indeed) is almost always rendered by καί γε. This is the result: "And he, meanwhile, has made the world, in all its seasonable beauty, and he has set eternity in their hearts" (Eccles. 3. 11, Knox translation, in footnote). σὺν τὰ πάντα ἐποίησεν καλὰ ἐν καιρῷ αὐτοῦ καί γε σὺν τὸν αἰῶνα ἔδωκεν ἐν καρδίᾳ αὐτῶν. As against this, some translators allowed themselves great liberty. The author of the Greek translation of Ecclesiasticus said in his Preface: "Hebrew words lose their force when they are translated into another language; moreover, when the Hebrews read out the law, the prophets and the other books among themselves, they read them out in a greatly different form."

The Greek of the book of Job supplies a good example of a version influenced by a different literary taste and spiritual temperament. It is shorter by about a fifth than the Hebrew, for the translator did not hesitate to abridge, to suppress repetitions and parallelisms which seemed to him unnecessary, to summarize or to rewrite some passages in a way more suited to his taste. In chapter 28, for example, he omits the vivid and picturesque description of the work of miners (verses 3, following; the Greek of this passage, as of that of similar omissions, was supplied by Origen from the translation of Theodotion, and the complete text is printed in most modern editions of the Septuagint without Origen's diacritical marks). He frequently cuts out metaphors, so that his book is less poetical and more didactic. Theological motives also played their part. He toned down or suppressed altogether such remarks of Job's as he thought blasphemous: so, 10. 3: "Is it well done in thee to play the tyrant?" became: ἢ καλόν σοι ἐὰν ἀσεβήσω; "Is it right for you if I am unrighteous?" To take another example, 9. 22: "Innocent and guilty, he sweeps all away", became: μέγαν καὶ δυνάστην ἀπολλύει ὀργή; "His anger destroys the great and the powerful." 27. 2: "As sure as he is a living God, he, the omnipotent, who so refuses me justice . . ." was weakened to: ζῆ κύριος ὃς οὕτω με κέκρικε; "He is a living God, who has thus judged me." He was clearly offended by words which seemed to question the righteous providence of God. So the impression made by the book as a whole is quite different: the dramatic debate between Job and God loses its bitter seriousness; Job is no longer the unjustly suffering innocent man who dares to demand an explanation of the Lord but the model of patience and humility who holds on above all to what he has always accepted and believed. Is there a less vital sense of the mystery of unjust suffering? Or is this more refined theological thinking? The translator seems to have changed the character of Job in the light of the acts of faith and resignation which occur at decisive moments in the poem, lessening in this way the torment of his divided spirit.

Even more instructive is a passage from the book of Isaias (25. 1–5), to which A. Coste has called attention.[5] Compare a fairly literal translation of the Greek text with the translation of the Hebrew given in the International Critical Commentary[6]:

> O Lord, my God,
> I shall extol thee, I shall praise thy name,
> For thou hast done wonderful things,
> An ancient design, a true one:
> May it come to be, O Lord.

> For you have brought cities down to heaps of rubble,
> Strong cities, so that their foundations fall;
> The city of the impious shall never be rebuilt for all eternity.

> Therefore the people that are beggared shall praise thee,
> And the cities of men suffering injustice shall praise thee,
> For thou hast become the helper of every humiliated city
> And a refuge for all who have lost heart because of their poverty.

> Thou deliverest them from wicked men,
> A refuge for the thirsty,
> And the inspiration of men suffering injustice.

> They will praise thee, as men of faint heart thirsting in Sion,
> Far from impious men, to whom thou hast given us over.

5 *Revue biblique*, 1954; p. 36.
6 *The Book of Isaiah*, vol. 1, by Arthur S. Peake, Edinburgh, 1912, and New York, Scribner, p. 425.

And from the Hebrew:

> Yahweh, thou art my God,
>   I will exalt thee, give thanks to thy name;
> For thou hast achieved wonders,
>   Plans (formed) long ago, in perfect faithfulness.

> For thou hast made the city a heap,
>   The fortified town a ruin;
> The palace of the "presumptuous". . .
>   It shall never more be built.

> Wherefore the strong people shall glorify thee,
>   The city of the awe inspiring shall fear thee;
> For thou hast been a stronghold to the poor,
>   A stronghold to the needy in his distress.

It can be seen how a number of slight changes, all in the same direction, as it were, have altered the tone of this text, bringing out a new spirit very close to that which emerges in the Gospel Beatitudes: the trusting and joyful humility of the "Poor of Israel", full of thankfulness for the benevolence of the God who had undertaken and would complete their deliverance.

It would be possible to multiply such examples, which show why the Septuagint must be studied today, especially the prophetic and sapiential books, for itself, and not simply for the better understanding of the Hebrew. It is not exaggerated to see in the Septuagint, as does A. Coste, "a link in the chain of Revelation". This study of the Greek Bible, as it reveals to us some aspects of the thought of the Jews of the Diaspora, just as the manuscripts discovered at Qumran throw light on certain currents of thought among Palestinian Jewry, can help us to achieve a better grasp of the stages of the slow preparation of men's souls for the coming of the Messias.

CHAPTER XI

THE NEW TESTAMENT

As we have it, the New Testament is a Greek work, but the fundamental problems it poses are analogous to those arising in the case of the Septuagint. Although they were written in Greek, the books that make up the New Testament were not, with the probable exception of the work of St Luke, written by men of Greek origin but by Jews who had become Christians. Besides this, the message to which these men bore witness and of which they were the first preachers was that of Jesus, who belonged, body and spirit, to Israel. Exegesis will therefore generally tend to uncover, under the Greek dress, thinking ruled by the categories of the Hebrew mind, and to hear again the echo of the words of Jesus himself, breaking through the barrier of time separating his life on earth from the composition of our Gospels. During the last fifty years an immense effort of exegesis has been directed to solving these problems. On the one hand, the problem of the "Semitic substrate" has been studied with great care in an attempt to read behind the Greek text, as it were like a watermark, the Aramaic expressions used by Jesus and his first disciples. On the other hand, all the details have been gathered together by means of which the exact sense can be determined of the essential vocabulary of the Christian message. Now at last a study has been begun which is as methodical as possible of the styles and literary genres both of the Gospels and the other apostolic writings.

THE SEMITISMS OF THE NEW TESTAMENT

The problem of the Aramaisms of the New Testament, which concerns only the Gospels, the first chapters of the Acts and the

Apocalypse, is exceedingly complex once one tries to go beyond a few very general statements. It is *a priori* likely that an oral catechism, which was at first in Aramaic, left some traces in our written Gospels; the evangelists themselves carefully preserved in their original tongue certain phrases used by Jesus (*Eli, Eli lamma sabachthani?* Matt. 27. 46). When it is known with what devotion the rabbinical writings preserved the "sayings of the Fathers", it can scarcely be doubted that the disciples of Jesus handed on their Master's words as literally as they could.[1] But once scientific accuracy is sought great difficulties are encountered, not the least of which is the lack of documents allowing any certain knowledge of the Aramaic dialect spoken by Jesus' contemporaries. We know now that the language of the Targums or translations of the Pentateuch and the prophets on which G. Dalman relied in his reconstruction of the "words of Jesus" was a somewhat artificial language, strongly influenced by Hebrew and also by Babylonian Aramaic. Doubtless the Aramaic manuscripts discovered at Qumran will throw new light on this question.

Nevertheless some critics have not hesitated to see in our Gospels the translation of works originally written in Aramaic. Moving on from theory to application, C. C. Torrey even published an English version[2] of the Aramaic text he thought it was possible to reconstruct. In this radical form his thesis has found few supporters. The contention of C. F. Burney[3] that there was an Aramaic original of the fourth Gospel has also met with lively opposition. The existence of Aramaic sources of the Apocalypse and the early chapters of the Acts is the subject of similar argument. The best book on the subject now is that

---

[1] A tradition, for which the oldest witness is Papias in the second century, presumes that there was a collection of *logia* or sayings, made by the apostle Matthew, in the Hebrew tongue, that is, in Aramaic. These *logia*, very likely linked with narrative, would have constituted the principal source of the Greek Gospel according to St Matthew.

[2] C. C. Torrey, *The Four Gospels: A New Translation*, 2nd edn, New York, Harper ,1947.

[3] C. F. Burney, *The Aramaic Origin of the Fourth Gospel*, Oxford and New York, Oxford Univ. Press, 1922.

of M. Black[4] whose careful and conservative conclusions, arrived at after minute analysis, can be regarded as established. The narrative portions of these works, in St Mark particularly, are clumsy and awkward in a way that may simply be the result of the bilingualism of the writer. As for the words of Jesus, although the parables have been for the most part rewritten in correct Greek, it seems most likely that for many of the isolated *logia* and for the discussions between Jesus and his disciples or adversaries, the evangelists used Aramaic sources, which their Greek faithfully follows.

Akin to this problem, but distinct from it, is that of the influence of the Septuagint, which arises especially in the case of St Luke's Gospel of the Childhood of Christ. It looks as though we are here faced with a deliberate intention to imitate the phraseology of the Greek Bible, in order to give to his narrative the style of Scripture. Scholars have written of intentional "Septuagintalisms" from a writer capable—as he shows he is in his prologue—of writing in the best Greek. Some critics, however, have been strongly opposed to the idea of such a pastiche, and have preferred to suppose that Luke incorporated a story more or less literally translated from the Hebrew, belonging to a Palestinian tradition. The question is one of the most discussed at the present day and it seems that it must remain unanswered. What is fairly plain is that the influence of the Septuagint makes itself felt in a vague way in all the books of the New Testament.

THE VOCABULARY OF THE NEW TESTAMENT

A spiritual revolution as profound as the birth of Christianity could not but betray itself in a new kind of language. Now that revolution was effected within the purely Judaic tradition, so that we should not be surprised to find the New Testament vocabulary at the same time so traditional and so new. We are today almost perfectly equipped with the tools for its study,

[4] M. Black, *An Aramaic Approach to the Gospels and Acts*, 2nd edn, Oxford and New York, Oxford Univ. Press, 1950.

wonderful tools provided for the exegete by English or German philology: concordances to the Hebrew Bible, to the Septuagint, to the New Testament, giving all the references for each word so that all the statistics and necessary comparisons can be made; a dictionary of the Greek of the papyri; a collection, still being made, of possible parallels in Hellenistic literature. Above all a group of German theologians, gathered together by G. Kittel and partially reformed after the war had taken its cruel toll of their number, is now near the completion of the publication of a theological vocabulary of the New Testament [5] in which the usage of each essential word is studied at length, in classical and Hellenistic Greek, in the Old Testament, both Hebrew and Greek, in Palestinian and Hellenistic Judaism and in the New Testament—a huge work, outstanding at the mid-century.

We cannot now embark on a detailed study, which would necessitate constant references to the texts, but a few examples must serve to show the importance and interest of such detailed scrutiny of the vocabulary. It is because the "justice of God" associated with his steadfastness and his mercy in the Old Testament does not mean or include the idea of punishment (when this idea is wanted the writers speak of God's "visits" or his "anger") that St Paul in his Epistle to the Romans can contrast the age of God's anger with the age of his justice (Rom. 1. 18 and 3. 21), and build on this plan of salvation realized in Christ his whole doctrine of "justification". It is because δόξα, which meant in Greek "honour", "reputation", had been used by the authors of the Septuagint to translate the Hebrew kâbhôd, "glory", "majesty" of God, and because they had further emphasized the idea of its spreading and saving power, that Luke, John and Paul were to be able to denote by this word the manifestation, to be seen from the beginning of his earthly life, and then blindingly present after the resurrection, of the divinity of Christ.

As for the spiritual content introduced by Christianity, the

[5] *Theologisches Wörterbuch zum Neuen Testament*, herausg. v. Gerhard Kittel (Stuttgart, 1933 on; in November, 1958, Bd vɪ, Lieferung 13 appeared, taking the work as far as προφήτης).

statistics speak for themselves. The Johannine writings use the word πιστεύειν, "believe", "have faith", about a hundred times, which is more than in the whole of the Old Testament. Paul, in his two epistles to the Romans and the Galatians, uses the word πίστις, "faith", nearly sixty times, here again more than in all the Old Testament. Ἀγάπη, "love", "charity", appears more then a hundred times in the work of John and Paul together, more than five times as often as in the Septuagint. There are also words significant by their absence: the two great Stoic virtues, ἀνδρεία, "courage", and καρτερία, "endurance", are not found once in the New Testament; but ἐλπίς, "hope", is found very many times, associated with faith and sustained by the trusting expectation of the whole tradition of the Bible. Paul, again, uses καυχᾶσθαι, "boast", "vaunt oneself", or nouns derived from it, fifty times to stigmatize pride and self-conceit. And need we do more than mention the association of χάρις καὶ εἰρήνη, "grace and peace", which is found at the beginning or at the end of almost all the epistles?

STYLES AND LITERARY GENRES

The interest now shown in the style of the writers of Scripture is no new or modern thing: already in the fifth century St Augustine, remembering that he had himself taught rhetoric at Rome and then at Milan, devoted some very interesting pages of the *De Doctrina Christiana* (Bk. III, ch. 7) to the eloquence of St Paul, applying to the study of two passages from his epistles (Rom. 5. 3–5; 2 Cor. 11. 16–30) all the resources of his old profession. But significant progress waited on the work of the German philologists. After the works of G. Norden on ancient literary prose and the language of Hellenistic religion,[6] M. Dibelius[7] and R. Bultmann[8] developed a method which

[6] G. Norden, *Die antike Kunstprosa vom VI Jahrhundert vor Christus bis in die Zeit der Renaissance* (Leipzig, 1916–18); *Agnostos Theos: Untersuchungen zur Formengeschichte religiöser Rede* (Leipzig and Berlin, 1929).

[7] M. Dibelius, *Die Formgeschichte des Evangeliums* (2nd edn, Tübingen, 1933).

[8] R. Bultmann, *Die Geschichte der synoptischen Tradition* (2nd edn, Göttingen, 1931).

was called in German *formgeschichtliche Methode* (Form-criticism), which consists in distinguishing by a consideration of stylistic characteristics the elements making up the records used by the evangelists from the literary forms in which the teaching and worship of the first Christian communities were expressed. Provided—though this has not always been the case—it is used with wisdom and not forced to conform to a rigidly systematic treatment, the method has shown itself effective. It seems to have made it possible to get over or beyond the synoptic problem, the problem of the relations between the Gospels, especially the first three, and to illuminate afresh the life of the Christian churches in the thirty years between Jesus' resurrection and the first Gospel writings.

SPEECH AND NARRATIVE IN THE GOSPELS

We have already seen that Aramaisms, which are very unevenly distributed through the Gospels, are common in the words spoken by our Lord. The teaching of the Master seems to be given there with such faithfulness to the latter that, despite the double translation, what we may perhaps be permitted to call his style is perceptible even in our English Bibles. Burney devoted a whole book[9] to studying the "poetry of our Lord", and Black confirmed and made more precise and specific his observations.[10] It is clear that Jesus followed the example of the prophets in formulating his message in oracular phraseology which could be easily memorized and handed on word for word, and he used for this purpose all the resources of Semitic poetry: parallelism, rhythm, assonance, rhyme, balanced grouping of strophes and so on. The best specialists, re-translating some of his words into Aramaic, go so far as to distinguish certain deliberately chosen sound effects, such as, for example, gutturals and sibilants to castigate the "hypocrites" (Matt. 6. 1–8), or liquids and labials to call to him "all those that labour and are burdened" (Matt. 11. 28–30).

[9] F. C. Burney, *The Poetry of Our Lord* (Oxford, 1925).
[10] *Op. cit.*

The isolated sayings of Jesus are deliberately given the form of the "proverbs" of the Old Testament, perennial truths expressed in striking images with, on his lips, a deepened meaning: "What is hidden, is hidden only so that it may be revealed; what is kept secret, is kept secret only that it may come to light" (Mark 4. 22). "It is not those who are in health that have need of the physician, it is those who are sick" (Mark 2. 17). "Salt is a good thing, but if the salt becomes tasteless, what will you use to season it with?" (Mark 9. 49).

The Beatitudes use a form common in the Psalms, many of which begin with the formula, "Blessed are they who . . ." The maledictions against the Pharisees recall those of Isaias (5. 8–24). The eschatological discourse of Mark 13 sets before us the same images as the prophets' descriptions of the "Day of Yahweh", associating cosmic catastrophes with the tribulations which mark on earth the visitation of God.

A good part of the teaching of Jesus is given in parables. Here again we are dealing with a literary form traditional in Israel, which later Rabbinism was to develop further. It would be superficial merely to admire the poetic spirit and the psychological acuteness they display, or their practical relevance to the everyday life of Palestinian peasants. If the word "parable" ($\pi\alpha\rho\alpha\beta\text{o}\lambda\dot{\eta}$) only means "comparison", the Hebrew word *māshāl* has a much more complex meaning: it is also a veiled reproach, ironical—as we see it in the "parable" of Nathan to David (2 Kings 12)—an enigma, which demands further explanation in order to be understood, like the dreams in the book of Daniel. Most of the parables concern the mystery of the Kingdom of God, its presence in the Person of Jesus, the conditions of entering into it, the contrast between its humble beginnings and its glorious growth. Veiled by allegories sometimes so simple and clear that those who listened could not fail to grasp the message, it was the immediate present crisis which was being revealed, the rejection of those who believed themselves called and the reception at the wedding feast of those who were thought to be excluded. Moreover it is fair and right to interpret the parables of the synoptic Gospels in the light of the sayings in which Jesus reveals himself in St John's Gospel, for in the fourth Gospel the glory of the risen Christ throws back a light on to all the acts of Jesus, so that all the accounts of these acts become signs revealing the Word and manifesting his glory: "I am the bread of life, the light of the world, the door of the sheepfold, the good shepherd, the true vine . . ."—these are still parables (John uses a synonym, παροιμία), but Jesus directly refers to himself in them, scandalizing his hearers, who did not understand or understood too much and were shocked and angry. In the closed circle of his disciples, in his last hours with them, Jesus was to explain himself more clearly, and when the Spirit came all things would be made plain.

It is difficult to set in their proper context most of the sayings of our Lord, for the evangelists inserted them at different moments during the course of their narrative or grouped them for didactic purposes. Some of them come at the end of short discussions: Jesus, disputing with his adversaries, most often Pharisees, ends the discussion with a definite declaration more or less explicitly asserting his claim to be the Messias. Mark 2. 1—3. 6 gives a grouped series of five arguments which appear to have been collected together purposely in order to bring out into the light the increasing opposition, at first secret ("they reasoned in their minds"), then indirect ("the Scribes and Pharisees . . . asked his disciples") and in the end direct to our Lord, ending in the decision to "make away with him". Perhaps five other disputes are collected in Mark 11. 27—12. 37; they are bracketed between the episodes of the cleansing of the Temple and the condemnation of the Scribes, and contain (12. 1-9) the all too clear parable of the murderous vine-dressers. It looks as though these writings, which are structurally much the same— legal or exegetical quibbles, snares set for Jesus to put him at odds with the Law or the Scriptures, battles of texts in the rabbinical manner—reflect the discussions of the first Christians when they had to justify their faith and explain their separatism to the Jews, by invoking particularly dramatic episodes in the life of their Master.

Some accounts tell how Jesus was to begin the Kingdom of

God, exorcizing devils and curing the sick, and how twice, at the baptism and at the transfiguration, God approved and guaranteed the work of his Son. At times stylized and arranged schematically,[11] at times rich in concrete details betraying the presence alongside the narrator of the eye-witness,[12] these accounts were chosen for their significance according to a general design, in which theology was no doubt more important than chronological exactitude and to the interpretation of which a speech of Peter's in the Acts gives us the key:

> You have heard the story, a story which ran through the whole of Judaea, though i t began in Galilee, after the baptism which John proclaimed; about Jesus of Nazareth, how God anointed him with the Holy Spirit and with power, so that he went about doing good, and curing all those who were under the devil's tyranny, with God at his side. We are witnesses of all he did in the country of the Jews, and in Jerusalem. And they killed him, hanging him on a gibbet; but on the third day God raised him up again. (Acts 10. 37–40.)

The occasion of Jesus' going up from Galilee to Jerusalem to die was clearly invested by the evangelists with a particular importance. Luke underlines this heavily when he says that Jesus—and here Luke departs from the order of events as they are given in Mark, which up to this point he has more or less constantly followed—"turned his eyes steadfastly towards the way that led to Jerusalem" (9. 51). The Greek text imitates here the Septuagint and says with exceptional solemnity: "Now it happened that in the time of the accomplishment of the days before his assumption he set his face firmly to go up to Jerusalem." The four evangelists end with the accounts of the passion and resurrection, which were probably very early settled and determined in their essential lines in order to be read during the commemoration of the pasch of our Lord.

[11] Cf., for example, Mark 1. 23–7; 4. 35–41.
[12] E.g., Mark 5. 21–43. It is known, not only from ancient tradition, but also from the actual witness of Peter (1 Peter 5. 13), that Mark was with him in Rome and helped him in his work.

PREACHING AND PRAYER IN THE EPISTLES

Just as scholars have sought especially to discover behind the Gospels, by a careful examination of literary forms, the way in which the first Christian communities preserved the memory of the words and acts of Jesus, so they have sought from the epistles not simply information on the different styles of their authors but some knowledge of the various forms taken by the preaching of the first century. The speeches reported in the Acts of the Apostles, in spite of their schematized form, do give us truly authentic examples of this preaching, but the study of the epistles surely allows us to know more.

A certain style can be seen in many passages of the epistles of St Paul, and also, with a less strongly marked individuality, in those of James and Jude and the second epistle of Peter; the relations of this style with that of the Stoic diatribe have been the object of detailed study by R. Bultmann since 1910. The diatribe is a form of moral exhortation developed especially in the Cynic and Stoic schools which found its most perfect form with Epictetus. It is a sort of compromise between the treatise and the dialogue, keeping the lively spontaneity and the alternately ironic and animated manner of the Socratic dialogue, with its short, abrupt phrasing, its breathless rhythm, its alliteration, antitheses, metaphors, personifications and method of arguing—all calculated to grip and arouse the reader, who is drawn into the discussion and himself tackled on this or that point, answered when he is supposedly objecting, and set thinking with questions. It is especially in the Epistle to the Romans that the marks of this style are discernible. The resemblance is most notable when Paul describes the reversal of values which the grace of Christ effects in the Christian, transforming slavery to sin into freedom in the Spirit, weakness into strength, suffering into joy, death into life.

Read two passages from the Second Epistle to the Corinthians (4. 8–13; 6. 4–10), the theme of which was splendidly taken up in a Christian work of the second century, the *Letter to Diognetus*; and then read these passages, the first from

Epictetus, the second from Plutarch, which portray, the first with admiration, the second ironically, the steadfastness of the Stoic sage when put to the test:

> Who, then, is a Stoic? . . . Show me a man who though sick is happy, though in danger is happy, though dying is happy, though condemned to exile is happy, though in disrepute is happy. Show him! By the gods, I would fain see a Stoic! (Epictetus, *Discourses*, Bk. ii, xix, 23-4; translated by W. A. Oldfather, in vol. ii of Loeb Classical Library edn, p. 267.)

> The Stoic Lapithes, as if forged of adamantine stuff by the dispassionateness of the sect, is not to be thought of as invulnerable or untouched by pain or sickness, but he does keep himself free from fear or grief or defeat or constraint, though he is wounded and racked with pain, or beholding the devastation of his native land or the sufferings of his fellow-citizens. When Pindar's Caeneus was thrown he was not injured, but the Stoic sage is different: when imprisoned, he is not confined; though cast from a cliff, cannot be forced against his will; though on the rack, is not tortured; though mutilated, unharmed; unconquered, though overthrown; besieged, but never taken; sold by the enemy, he is still invincible. (Plutarch, *Moralia*, 1057 D–E; Teubner edn, vol. vi, fasc. 2, Leipzig, 1952, ed. M. Pohlenz; p. 59.)

It is true that the spiritual atmosphere is infinitely different, but the style is the same: the same rhythms and the same sort of details, paronomasia and alliteration which translation cannot preserve. Paul would have been able to hear such exhortations in the Hellenistic cities, but it is also certain that such oratorical methods had found their way into the synagogues of the Diaspora and Paul had doubtless learned them there.

A Greek would not have felt himself in a strange land had he read the two passages just mentioned from 2 Corinthians or, for example, the first two chapters of the Epistle to the Romans. But he would have done reading from the fourth chapter onwards, or if he had glanced at the third chapter of Galatians, or the third chapter of the same Epistle to the Corinthians.

For there he would have come upon a style of argument
deeply rooted in Jewish soil, which later rabbinical exegesis
developed considerably under the name of *Midrash*, the detailed study of Scriptural texts in order to find in them the
meaning of contemporary events. The unjustified contempt in
which rabbinical literature used to be held—sometimes it was
even described as so much rubbish—prevented for a long time
the use of these writings to shed light on the New Testament.
Their excessive use of allegorical interpretation does, it is true,
tend to put off the western mind. But this is a kind of writing
and interpretation having its source in the Bible itself. The nub of
the argument is that God is reliable, that he does not regret his
promises, that his acts reveal a planned progression that is not
broken by the chaos of history. The best way of understanding
the present is therefore to examine the Book in which the
inspired writers have reported the words of God and explained
the events of the past in their light. So the deliverance from
Egypt throws its light forward on to the return from Babylon
and on to Messianic times. It is in this way, for example, that
Ezechiel 16 explains the imminent destruction of Jerusalem by
placing it in the context of the broken covenant, and promises
God's pardon, taking texts from Deuteronomy, Osee and
Jeremias. Now read chapters 9–11 of the Epistle to the Romans:
confronted with the problem of the rejection of Israel, so tragic
for him that Paul says: "It has ever been my wish that I myself
might be doomed to separation from Christ, if that would
benefit my brethren, my own kinsmen by race"; so troubled, he
appeals to a succession of texts to make sense of the apparent
failure of God's plan and to be able to prophesy the eventual
salvation of his people, the "Israelites, adopted as God's sons;
the visible presence, and the covenant, and the giving of law, and
the Temple worship, and the promises, are their inheritance;
the patriarchs belong to them, and theirs is the human stock
from which Christ came" (9. 3–5). There is the source of the
typological exegesis by means of which the first generation of
Christians could understand Jesus in the light of the great figures
of Israel's past. The Fathers of the Church were to use this

method very widely in their homilies on the Scripture. It is
rather too often mixed with much allegorical interpretation,
especially in the Alexandrian Fathers who were influenced by
Philo; but this should not prevent the recognition of a well-
established traditional method, the systematic study of which
would help towards greater understanding of the New Testament.

Preaching and teaching cannot be considered apart from
prayer: "May all the wealth of Christ's inspiration have its
shrine among you; now you will have instruction and advice
for one another, full of wisdom, now there will be psalms, and
hymns and spiritual music, as you sing with gratitude in your
hearts to God" (Col. 3. 16). In the tradition of the prophets
and psalmists prayer took on naturally the form of a doxology,
and there are many such in the epistles. Thanksgivings, εὐλογίαι,
often developed into long benedictions, which listed the glorious
revelations of God and the blessings granted to his people. In
the Greek these become relative or participial phrases which
follow one another in a sort of balanced way, carefully composed rhythmically; so Ps. 102 (103):

> Bless the Lord, my soul, unite, all my powers, to bless that holy
> name.
> Bless the Lord, my soul, remembering all he has done for thee,
> how he pardons all thy sins,
> heals all thy mortal ills,
> rescues thy life from deadly peril,
> crowns thee with the blessings of his mercy;
> how he contents all thy desire for good,
> restores thy youth, as the eagle's plumage is restored. . . .

This hymnodic style can often be found in St Paul's epistles,
and it may be that we can catch there the echo of the liturgical
prayers recited or chanted in the earliest congregations.

Moreover, these are hymns to Christ, in which can be seen
confessions of faith, expressing the sovereignty of the Lord, or
the essentials of the Christian "mystery". Such are, for example, the hymn to Christ brought down to death on the cross

and raised by the Father (Phil. 2. 6–11), or the hymn to Christ as "the true likeness of the God we cannot see" and as "that head whose body is the Church" (Col. 1. 15–20). Here we can see in its origins the full, solemn language of the liturgy, in which the Church was to compose its eucharistic prefaces.

CHAPTER XII

GREEK AS THE LANGUAGE
OF THE CHURCH

Can we still talk of a "sacred language" when it is no longer a matter of the books containing the Revelation, but of the works of Christian writers of the early centuries? Many of them have been called Fathers of the Church; some of their works— the *Shepherd* of Hermas, the Epistle of Barnabas, the letter of Clement of Rome to the Corinthians—are even found included in some of the most ancient manuscripts of the New Testament and were once regarded as inspired Scripture. The most famous of the Fathers, Origen (who is, however, still the object of a good deal of discussion), Basil of Caesarea, Gregory of Nyssa and many others, not to mention the Latin Fathers, were held, down to the late Middle Ages, to have received a special grace of inspiration. "The Fathers", says St John Damascene, "are inspired by the Spirit. . . . It is by the Holy Spirit that the Law spoke, and the prophets, the evangelists, the priests and the doctors of the Church." The strict return to the Scriptures alone preached by the Reformers, and the precise decrees of the Council of Trent, have led to a careful distinction being drawn between the divine word and human words, however authoritative. Nevertheless the common agreement of the Fathers enjoins that the Church shall be the interpreter of the Scriptures and that the definitions of ecumenical councils are rules of faith: did not Gregory the Great and others after him compare with the four Gospels the four great councils of Nicaea, Constantinople, Ephesus and Chalcedon?

It is not part of our present study to consider Greek Christian literature. We should merely like to show, by referring to a few precise points, the contribution of the Greek language in the definition of dogma and the description of the spiritual life.[1]

Sometimes voices have been raised against this "Helleniza-tion" of Christian thought: the message, it is said, loses in purity what it gains in its ability to reach a wider audience. A fruitless opposition, which would have ended by depriving revelation of its universal relevance by denying it the power to suit the forms of its expression to the mental habits of the different peoples to whom it has one after the other been declared. When it was thought over by minds formed by Greek culture the Word of God could not but be expressed in a new voice. It is not without importance that Origen attended the lectures of Ammonius Saccas, the master of Plotinus and the founder of Neo-Platonism, or that Basil of Caesarea and Gregory Nazian-zen frequented the schools of Athens, or that John Chrysostom learned the rules of rhetoric from Libanius. Yet Origen's thought, whatever its bold unorthodoxy, is always governed by an intense devotion to the person of Jesus which led him in the end to martyrdom; Basil and Gregory were the great defenders of the faith of Nicaea; and John Chrysostom used all the resources of his rhetoric in the service of St Paul. It is true that leaving Paul and John and opening, let us say, the *Protrepticus* of Clement of Alexandria, gives the impression of moving into a different atmosphere: see with what youthful ardour he quotes, mixed with his texts from the Scriptures, from the Iliad and the Odyssey, Hesiod, Pindar and Plato—clearly he is speaking to a different audience. But he is not delivering a different message. One sentence defines the intention of the first Christian doctor to address the intellectual élite of the Greek world: "Come . . . I will show thee the Word, and the mysteries of the Word, expounding them after thine own fashion."[2]

---

[1] On the use of the Greek language in the Christian liturgy, see the work on eastern liturgies, in this series.

[2] Clement of Alexandria, *Protrepticus*, ch. 12, in translation of W. Wilson, in vol. IV of the Ante-Nicene Christian Library, Edinburgh, 1868; p. 107.

THE PRECISE STATEMENT OF DOCTRINE

The transcendence and providence of God

When Christianity came into contact with paganism, it was not faced with any really coherent philosophical system but by a kind of vague, popular philosophy, in which eastern gnosticism was mingled with Stoic pantheism and cosmological speculations derived from Plato's *Timaeus*. Its dominant note was one of fatalism, the determination by fate of the world and of human life. Confronted by the forces of nature, the implacable determinism of which was shown forth in the unchanging courses of the stars, which were held to be gods, human freedom seemed to find refuge only in defiantly asserting at least some sort of autonomy or in a feverish desire for salvation which the mystery religions could not truly satisfy. It was the "philosophizing, with empty phantasies drawn from human tradition", to which in his Epistle to the Colossians St Paul opposes the headship of Christ.

The first task of the Fathers was therefore the maintenance of the unity, transcendence and providence of God. Basing their teaching on the Bible, they emphasized the gulf separating God from the created world, while at the same time stressing the paternal care God shows for that world by his willing assumption of humanity in the Person of his Son. Against idolatry, against the Gnostics who multiplied like mythology the number of beings mediating between God and our world, against the Stoics who imagined God to be a kind of living fiery matter within the world, the Fathers firmly and plainly asserted the uniqueness of God. Between him, the only uncreated being (ἀγένητος), incorruptible (ἄφθαρτος) and immortal (ἀθάνατος), and created things (τὰ γένητα), there is an absolute separation, which the Bible calls *holiness* and which they characterized by the word *transcendence* (ὑπεροχή). True, the divine presence pervades, upholds and governs the universe, but it is not spatially contained (ἀχώρητος). And they were to go on using more and more negative terms to set God beyond our created,

finite grasp; St John Chrysostom even devoted a whole treatise
to the "incomprehensibility" of God (Περὶ τοῦ ἀκαταλήπτου).

But in making man in his own likeness God granted that he
should share by grace in his incorruptibility and immortality.
Far from leaving man cut off from himself God has been with
him, even after he sinned, on his journey through the ages,
guiding him according to his providence, according to his plan
for man's salvation which the Fathers, following St Paul
(Ephes. 1. 3–14), called by the very Greek word "economy"
(οἰκονομία), meaning by that both the stages of revelation and
at the same time the Incarnation itself. And just as they were
clear that there could be no natural ascent to God, so also they
proclaimed the glorious future opened to us by the Redemption,
even using, to describe the state of man redeemed, the word
"deification" (θεοποίησις).

The theology of the Son of God

So long as Christianity developed in Jewish surroundings
the faith of Christ had only to use, in its expression and defence,
the categories of Jewish thought as they were to be found
particularly in the prophetic books of the Old Testament;
terms, that is, such as "Messias" and "Servant of the Lord",
which were at first used as titles of Jesus. Early on, however,
the latter dropped out of use except in liturgical formulas,
and the first, which was translated into Greek as Χριστός,
and would have had an alien sound to Greek ears, very
soon lost its Messianic overtones and became almost a proper
noun on its own or in close association with the name of
Jesus.

A primitive and somewhat crude attempt at Trinitarian
theology can be found in some works of Judaeo-Christian
origin, and especially in the *Shepherd* of Hermas. The Son and
the Holy Spirit are described as "Angels" and sometimes named
as Michael and Gabriel; or they are associated with the
seraphim of Isaias' vision of the glory of God (ch. 6). But these
ways of speaking, sprung from Jewish apocalyptic but unintelligible to the Greek mind, were to give place to the theology of

the divine Persons, to which their clumsiness is only very distantly related. It is clear that the theology of the Son of God developed after New Testament times along quite a different line. The names which were most commonly used, *Kyrios* and *Logos*, although they were deeply rooted in Biblical tradition, awoke important echoes in the Greek mind. *Kyrios* called to mind the sovereign kingship of Christ, opposing it to the claims of the Caesars, and his divinity, by associating it with Yahweh. *Logos* meant both the Word of God, creating the world and guiding its history, and the divine Reason, immanent in the universe and participated in by all rational creatures.

And it was from the book of Wisdom, written in an intellectual environment already profoundly Hellenized, that St Paul and the author of the Epistle to the Hebrews borrowed the terms which so often recur in the works of the Alexandrian doctors, by which the sacred writer described the divine Wisdom: "Steam (ἀτμίς) that ascends from the fervour of divine activity, pure effluence (ἀπόρροια) of his glory who is God all-powerful, she feels no passing taint; she, the glow (ἀπαύγασμα) that radiates from eternal light, she, the untarnished mirror (ἔσοπτρον) of God's majesty, she, the faithful image (εἰκών) of his goodness" (Wisdom 7. 25–6).

One God in three Persons

The grievous crisis provoked by Arianism, in which the imperial authority was also concerned, forced the bishops of the Church, whose unity was threatened for several decades, to define precisely the relations of the Father and the Son in the Trinity. But when we approach the technical language of dogmatic definitions we must be careful not to gain a false impression: patristic writings are not as a whole the works of controversialists but of preachers, so that spirituality, and commentaries on the Scriptures, play a greater part than scholastic argument. It was only reluctantly and in self-defence that the Fathers had recourse to philosophical categories for the expression of Christian mysteries, because the heretics first abused these means, "(perverting) with the technical terminology of this kind . . . the simplicity and artlessness of the faith".[3]

Playing on the vagueness of two words which the philosophers seem never to have distinguished ($\dot{\alpha}\gamma\acute{\epsilon}\nu\eta\tau\sigma\varsigma$, "uncreated", and $\dot{\alpha}\gamma\acute{\epsilon}\nu\nu\eta\tau\sigma\varsigma$, "unbegotten"), the Arians claimed that since the Father alone is unbegotten we cannot say that the Son is, as he is, uncreated ($\dot{\alpha}\gamma\acute{\epsilon}\nu\eta\tau\sigma\varsigma$): he is therefore only the first of all creatures. At the Council of Nicaea (325) the Fathers defined the dogma in the formulas now found in the Creed in the Mass: $\gamma\epsilon\nu\nu\eta\theta\acute{\epsilon}\nu\tau\alpha$, $o\dot{v}$ $\pi o\iota\eta\theta\acute{\epsilon}\nu\tau\alpha$, $\dot{o}\mu o o\acute{v}\sigma\iota o\nu$ $\tau\hat{\omega}$ $\Pi\alpha\tau\rho\acute{\iota}$ (genitum, non factum, consubstantialem Patri); and to make sure there was no doubt they explicitly condemned the familiar formulas of Arius: $\mathring{\eta}\nu$ $\pi o\tau\epsilon$ $\mathring{o}\tau\epsilon$ $o\mathring{v}\kappa$ $\mathring{\eta}\nu$, $\dot{\epsilon}\xi$ $o\mathring{v}\kappa$ $\mathring{o}\nu\tau\omega\nu$ $\dot{\epsilon}\gamma\acute{\epsilon}\nu\epsilon\tau o$, "there was a time when he was not, he came into being from what was not". By using the word "consubstantial" the Council of Nicaea asserted that there was between the Father and the Son not merely a community of nature—as between two individuals of the same species—but identity of essence. It was only after considerable struggle that the word was generally imposed.

It remained to define with more precision the distinctness of the divine Persons. This is the extremely complicated story of the word $\dot{v}\pi\acute{o}\sigma\tau\alpha\sigma\iota\varsigma$, hypostasis. The word was a recent importation into the philosophical vocabulary and meant concrete, objective, distinct reality, as opposed to appearance. Literally translated into Latin it is substantia, and it appeared in the anathemas of Nicaea as a synonym for $o\dot{v}\sigma\acute{\iota}\alpha$, ousia. Now Origen and his pupils had used it to denote the separate existence of the Father and the Son, so that many of the eastern Fathers spoke of three hypostases. The word was suspect to the Latins, who interpreted it as three substances, and saw in it a threat to the unity of God. The Greeks, for their part, were loth to accept the word $\pi\rho\acute{o}\sigma\omega\pi o\nu$, the literal translation of the Latin persona, which seemed to them, since it meant a mask, a dramatic character or part, insufficient to express the distinction of Persons. Thus the lack of parallels in the Greek and Latin

[3] St Basil, On the Spirit, ch. 6 (trans. Rev. Blomfield Jackson, in vol. VIII of the Nicene and Post-Nicene Fathers, 2nd Series; Oxford, 1895; p. 8).

vocabularies, or worse, their purely verbal parallelism, was added to the ambiguity of the language of philosophy. It was only after the work of clarification carried out especially by the Cappadocians, Basil of Caesarea and Gregory Nazianzen, that the Council of Chalcedon (451) was able to impose the definitive Greek formula: *one substance, three hypostases, μία οὐσία, τρεῖς ὑποστάσεις.*[4]

THE EXPRESSION OF THE LIFE OF THE SPIRIT

The life of the spirit is most often referred to in the Bible by the metaphor of *walking*: "A multitude of peoples will make their way to it, crying, Come, let us climb up to the Lord's mountain peak, to the house where the God of Jacob dwells; he will teach us the right way, we will walk in the paths he has chosen" (Isaias 2. 3). And St Luke shows us Zachary and Elizabeth "following (lit., walking in, πορευόμενοι ἐν) all the commandments and observances of the Lord without reproach". Paul uses the verb περιπατεῖν more than thirty times, always in this metaphorical sense. So the life of the spirit is opposed to the life of nature (Rom. 8. 4–9). Love, *agapê*, is the "way which is better than any other" (1 Cor. 12. 31), which defines the "Christian way of life"—for English has preserved this metaphor. And the Jews call the juridical commentary on the Law *halakhah*, from *halakh*, "to walk", "go".

It was among the Jewish Christians that there developed during the second century the idea of the "two ways"; its origins might perhaps be traced back to Deuteronomy (30. 15) or to Jeremias (21. 8): "And this warning the Lord gives to the common folk: Here is choice I offer you between life and death, take which course you will." The manual of discipline of the community of Qumran contains a long development of this

[4] Read St Basil, Letter 38 (in vol. 1 of the Loeb Classical Library edn, translated by R. J. Deferrari, 1926), on the distinction between substance and hypostasis. The awkwardness of the explanation's technique, because of the want of any really satisfactory comparisons, is strongly in contrast with the vigour with which the faith is affirmed. In the Middle Ages the Latin theologians translated hypostasis by *subsistentia* to avoid ambiguity.

theme, in which the opposition of the two spirits is emphasized especially, perhaps because of Persian influence: two kinds of men stand opposed to one another in the world until the Judgement, those ruled by the spirit of perversity and those inspired by the spirit of truth. In two related forms which clearly betray their common origin two Judaeo-Christian works treat of the same idea, the *Didache* and the letter of Pseudo-Barnabas. The theme is made great use of in the *Shepherd* of Hermas and is found again in patristic tradition, to inspire in the end the "rules for the discernment of spirits". To live according to the flesh or according to the Spirit, to be children of light or children of darkness, that is, in Pauline or Johannine terms, the choice offered to the Christian. The ways of God are not our ways, and being a Christian implies a breaking away, a conversion. The Christian spiritual life is here being lived in the world of the mind of Israel, dominated by memories of the removal of Abraham from his native land to gain the land that God would show him, of the exodus of the Hebrew people from the land of their bondage, and of their crossing the desert led by the pillar of cloud towards the Promised Land. Man is a traveller—*homo viator*—or rather, a pilgrim, walking under the guidance of God.

There is another idea, which came into being in Alexandria under the influence of Philo, which the Fathers of the Church were to use a great deal, the idea of likeness, of imitation. There are few examples as significant of the way in which Christian thinkers assimilated all that was best in the Greek tradition. In the *Theaetetus*, having shown how the true lover of wisdom is unarmed in the struggles here below, Plato warns him that he must flee this world: "Wherefore we ought to fly away from earth to heaven as quickly as we can; and to fly away is to become like God, as far as this is possible; and to become like him, is to become holy and just and wise" (176; trans. B. Jowett). Looking forward to death, which will set the soul free from the "prison" of the body, a constant effort of purification (κάθαρσις) can release the mind from the deceptions of sensible images and accustom it to the contemplation of the Ideas, the only true reality, and of that one which governs all of them, the Idea of the Good, which, itself beyond being, is the source and the end of all that exists. Clement of Alexandria found an echo of revelation in this and added a text from St Paul: "And openly and expressly the apostle, in the first Epistle to the Corinthians, says, 'Be ye followers of me, as also I am of Christ' (1 Cor. 11. 1), in order that that may take place. If ye are of me, and I am of Christ, then ye are imitators of Christ, and Christ of God." [5]

Remembering the verse of Genesis, "And God said, Let us make man, wearing our own image and likeness" (1. 26), and re-thinking it in their Platonist way, Clement, Origen and Gregory of Nyssa were often to develop this theme with different shades of interpretation. Since man possesses intelligence, he is created in the likeness of God; when God breathed life into him he gave him a share in his Spirit and called him to imitate him: from inceptive likeness to complete resemblance, that is the way for man. But the mist of sin tarnishes the mirror wherein God is reflected, and without destroying the spiritual nature of the soul it takes away the divine vision, at the same time annulling the promises of immortality and overwhelming the soul once more in the animal nature of man. Baptism restores to the Christian his likeness to God, but it is left to him to perfect it, by purifying practices, in order to attain to the fullness of the original image. Thus the course ideally suggested by Plato becomes a realizable vocation, for we know that man was indeed created in the image of God and that the grace which marked him at his beginning grants also that he shall come at last to the end. So a Platonic phrase, illuminated by the revealed Word, can express the stages of the "supernatural life".

When we draw up the account of the relations between Christian and Greek thought, we are brought to the conclusion that not only did the faith gain from it but Hellenism lost nothing by it either. Under the compulsion to satisfy the requirements of clarity so deeply natural to the Greek mind the

---

[5] *Stromata*, Book II, ch. 22; translated by W. Wilson, in vol. XII of the Ante-Nicene Christian Library, Edinburgh, 1869; p. 77.

Fathers of Alexandria, Antioch and Cappadocia made a great stride towards the understanding of the faith and also made sure, at the cost of many struggles, that a real theology should arise. On the other hand, we may wonder whether they did not contribute to Hellenism much more than they borrowed from it. By giving to the old Platonist tradition a new life-blood they saved it from a sort of debasement that its popularity might have doomed it to. Later in the same way Dionysius the Areopagite and the mystics who used and followed him, in their development of a negative theology concerned with safeguarding the transcendence of the ineffable God, saved Plotinus' Neo-Platonism from foundering in a welter of theurgical superstition. The early Christian theologians, measuring against the standard of the revelation of the Logos the partial truths which they found in pagan thought, ensured what could not perhaps have been expected without them, the survival, and later the renaissance, of Greek thought. And so became true the assertions made, about the year 200, by two Christian writers of Alexandria:

"What the soul is in the body, that the Christians are in the world." [6]

"Wherefore, since the Word himself has come to us from heaven, we need not, I reckon, go any more in search of human learning to Athens and the rest of Greece, and to Ionia. For if we have as our teacher him that filled the universe with his holy energies in creation, salvation, beneficence, legislation, prophecy, teaching, we have the Teacher from whom all instruction comes; and the whole world, with Athens and Greece, has already become the domain of the Word." [7]

[6] *The Epistle to Diognetus*, ch. 6, translated by J. A. Kleist, p. 139, in No. 6 of "Ancient Christian Writers", London, Longmans, Green and Co., and Westminster, Md, Newman Press, 1948.

[7] Clement of Alexandria, *Exhortation to the Heathen*, ch. 11, translated by W. Wilson, *op. cit.*, vol. IV, p. 100.

PART III

LATIN
by Albert Blaise

CHAPTER XIII

HISTORICAL SKETCH OF CHRISTIAN LATIN

When we are considering Latin, the words "sacred language" immediately call to mind the Latin of the liturgy, and especially that of the prefaces and collects; that is, a language of worship, in some regards a priestly language. But there is in liturgical Latin an important element of Biblical Latin, which is also a sacred language. On the other hand the language of the Fathers of the Church, the language of theology, of what is called sacred literature as opposed to secular or profane literature, was not different in its essentials from Biblical or liturgical Latin. At the end of the Roman Empire, the Christian writers had created a sort of common tongue somewhat different from that used by secular or pagan authors. And this tradition has been preserved, at least in vocabulary, in spite of the changes it suffered in the Middle Ages and the humanist reaction that followed the Renaissance. It is that language, which was more or less established by the end of the Roman Empire, that we intend to describe here.

It used to be called "Church Latin"; it was for many people simply a variation of late or vulgar Latin. This is no longer so. More than a century ago Ozanam discerned the revolution, almost, in the history of Latin brought about by Christianity. Pius IX, in his letter to Cardinal d'Avanzo (April 1st, 1875), congratulated him on having restored the honour of Christian Latin, *decus Christianae latinitatis*, which many used to regard as a corruption of classical Latin, *quam multi corruptionis insimularunt veteris sermonis,* when it was on the contrary a reformation of the language made necessary by the introduction of the Christian faith: *dum patet linguam . . . necessario novam induere debuisse formam post invectam a Christo legem.* The progress of linguistic studies now enables us to form a more accurate estimate of the way the language has evolved.

First there were the works, in the last century, of Roensch, Koffmane, Goelzer and Bonnet; and more recently hundreds of monographs have been produced on this kind of Latin. We might mention particularly the many studies published by the Catholic University of Washington in the series, *Patristic Studies,* and those of the school of Nijmegen, founded thirty years ago by Mgr J. Schrijnen and continued at present by Christine Mohrmann; besides the journal *Vigiliae Christianae,* a series of works has been published on the Latin of the Fathers in a collection entitled: *Latinitas Christianorum primaeva.*

All these studies have given us a more precise idea of what is now called Christian Latin. If some linguists are not agreed that it constitutes a separate, special language, properly speaking, nevertheless its profound originality has been recognized. Christianity brought about a sort of revolution in the history of the Latin language; this "baptized" Latin strikes us as a different language from that of profane authors; it is the language of Christian people, a language which over ten centuries preserved the unity of western Europe.

But it is no easy thing to give an idea of this great phenomenon, in all its diversity. A library of classical Latin books could be held in a few bookcases; for that of Christian Latin almost a whole building would be needed. Besides, it is not all of equal importance nor has it all an equal value. This is why we can perhaps achieve our end by contenting ourselves with a presentation of Christian Latin as it was at the end of the Roman Empire. The authors of this period served always as models for later ages, and St Augustine became a sort of classic, just as the Leonine Sacramentary to a large extent determined the language of the liturgy. And first of all it would be as well briefly to sketch out the history of this sort of Latin.

THE BEGINNINGS

The beginnings of Christian Latin are unrecorded and ante-date its first appearance in written works. We must remember that Christianity was brought to Rome as it was brought into other Mediterranean ports, by hellenized Jews, and it spread first among the proletariat of the city. Worship was then in Greek, and it was the Greek Bible that was read. But the need to translate the good tidings into Latin grew as more and more of the city's Latin-speaking poor accepted the new faith. To judge from the manuscripts that have survived and by the quotations in the patristic writings of the third century, these first translations must have been many and varied both in Rome and in Africa. According to St Augustine[1] everyone who felt himself at all capable of making such a translation felt driven to do so by his proselytizing zeal. Now these first African and Roman translations are notable for their extreme care to pre-serve the letter of the sacred text. This leads to many important consequences, the first being a strongly exotic quality both in vocabulary and syntax. The traditional literary convention forbade the use of borrowings from foreign languages except with very great caution. Nothing of this kind is found in these translations, and Greek terms (as well as a few Hebrew ones such as *pascha, amen,* etc.) crowded into the language of the first Latin Christians. Most of them were to become permanently established, such as *ecclesia, episcopus, baptisma* (*baptismus*); others were more suspect: for example, *caritas* (or *dilectio*) and *gratia* were to replace *agapê* and *charisma*; some were to persist alongside of Latin words: for example, *diaconus* and *minister, ethnici* and *gentiles*; and others again never had Latin equiva-lents except in the poets; *anathema, angelus, eucharistia,* etc. Complete figures are impossible to give because of the lack of information, but we may guess that more than half of the Greek words imported into Latin Christian usage date from this first period of translation; that is, from the second century.

---

[1] *De doctrina Christiana*, 2, 11, 16; in Migne, *Patrologia Latina*, 34, col. 43 (hereafter quoted as Migne, P.L., followed by volume and column number).

Parallel with this invasion of Greek words there went the creation of many neologisms in Latin. These were made with no concern for the purity of the language, especially in the cases of nouns in *-tio*, *-tor*, and verbs in *-ficare*. Christine Mohrmann ("Traits caractéristiques du latin des chrétiens", *Miscellanea Mercati* I, Vatican, 1946, p. 437) has noted that the Greek terms were kept on the whole for the concrete aspects—institutions (e.g. *eucharistia, baptismus*), the hierarchy (e.g. *episcopus, presbyter, diaconus*)—while Latin neologisms were created, or old words used in a new sense, to express abstract or spiritual ideas like redemption or salvation; e.g. *sanctificatio*, a new word to translate ἁγιασμός; *confessio*, an older word taking on a new sense to correspond to the ἐξομολόγησις of the Septuagint, and no longer simply "declaration" or "avowal" but "recognition of the greatness of God, praise" and so "affirmation of belief", etc.[2] Some of these literal transfers from Greek to Latin seem to us surprising and almost slavish, such as *supersubstantialis* to correspond to ἐπιούσιος; yet it remains in our Vulgate (Matt. 6. 11), while the Father of the liturgy used the word *quotidianus* he found in the text of Luke (11. 3).

The extreme care for the letter of which we have spoken led the translators to follow the sacred text very closely and depart as little as possible from a word for word rendering. This introduced a certain number of Hellenisms, or at least some constructions unknown in the literary language. Particularly to be noted are noun clauses introduced by *quod, quia, quoniam*, instead of the accusative and infinitive construction, corresponding to the Greek ὅτι clauses; *si* used in indirect questions for *num*, "whether": *videre si, interrogare si*, "to see if, to ask if"; the infinitive of purpose, like *venimus adorare*, "we have come to worship" (Matt. 2. 2): the Codex Vercellensis (John 6. 52) even preserves for us an example in which this infinitive is

[2] The same phenomenon appears again later: the advent, the manifestation of Christ, is called *apparentia* in Tertullian, *manifestatio* in St Augustine and St Jerome, *apparitio* in St Leo and others; but the Greek word *epiphania* always denotes the feast that celebrates this manifestation.

preceded by *ad*—*dare ad manducare*, "to give to eat"—which
clearly betrays the popular character of this text.

Another aspect of these first translations is their common,
everyday character: those who made them were writing for the
common folk, and not having themselves attended the schools
of the orators they professed some scorn for such manners. It
was just this uncouth impression made by the sacred books that
put off the scholars of that period and invited their sarcasm. We
have later witnesses to this, at the time when Christian writers
wanted to produce literary works and yet proclaimed that they
preferred truth to eloquence, respect for the holy text with all
its crudity to the splendour of profane letters. It was for them
truly a matter of a sacred language, not only because it en-
shrined revelation and mystery, but also because it was forbidden
to alter it: *idiomata scripturae divinae nulla praesumptione
temeretis* (*De institutione divinarum literarum*, c. 15; Migne,
P.L., 70, 1126C), "do not with any presumption desecrate
the expressions properly belonging to divine Scripture", said
Cassiodorus. St Augustine accepted—and that not only in his
sermons—the barbarism *floriet* (instead of *florebit*) because that
future was attested in the versions of the Bible that he used
(e.g. Ps. 131. 18, quoted in *De doctrina christiana*, II, 13, 20;
Migne, P.L., 34, 45). St Jerome preserved in his new translation, which later became the Vulgate, a large number of
popular words belonging to the primitive versions, such as
subsannare, "to mock"; *manducare* in the sense of *edere, come-
dere*, "to eat"; *eructare*, which had taken on the meaning "to
utter, declare". Indeed, these popular terms had become in a
way hallowed and solemnized by being regularly heard in
readings from the Bible.

Now there are still surviving some other remains of the
Latin of the early Christians. The ancient Latin versions of the
Letter of St Clement to the Corinthians and of the *Didache*,
as well as the so-called "Vulgate" version of the *Shepherd* of
Hermas, all date from the same period, probably from the first
half of the second century. These writings betray the influence
already being felt of the first translations of the Bible. They

show the same popular character, as well as an extreme literalism in their quotations from the Scriptures. To these must be added a few Roman and African inscriptions and the Acts of the martyrs of Scillium in Africa (180 A.D.), though these last only consist in four or five pages of text.

THE FIRST WRITINGS OF A LITERARY CHARACTER

More important is the *Passio SS. Perpetuae et Felicitatis* (martyred in 203). It has sometimes been attributed to Tertullian, though only the grandiloquent prologue could come from his pen. We have a contemporary Greek translation of the account itself, which was written in a Latin not popular, but everyday, which was to become the Latin of hagiographic literature: its naïve simplicity sometimes makes us feel that we are already reading the Golden Legend. Much more than the *Octavius* of Minucius Felix, who in his classical purism scarcely risked a few Christian terms, this *Passio* gives us some idea of the language of the Christians of the beginning of the third century.

From the grammatical point of view, let us note for example the use of the partitive *de*: *de aqua bibere*; compound prepositions: *desub ipsa scala*; *noceo* used with an accusative, which was due to the influence of translation-literature; nouns in apposition being used as adjectives: *presbyterum doctorem*. To the everyday Latin of the time belong such expressions as *se mittere in aliquem* or *ad pedes alicuius*, "to throw oneself at or at the feet of someone"; *orationem facere* in place of *orare*; nouns like *sufferentia* for *patientia*, *concussura* for *concussio*. Christian terms are particularly numerous in the prologue; they had been introduced by the first translators of the Bible and all of them can be found in Tertullian. Notable among them are: *aedificatio, gloria, gratia, instrumentum* (in the sense of "teaching, instruction"; after Tertullian it also meant "Scripture"), *virtus* in the sense of "power". In the body of the work we note, for example, *dejicare*, "to cause to apostatize"; *petere, postulare, rogare*, in the sense of "pray"; *refrigerare*, "to comfort";

manducare with eucharistic overtones; *magnificare*, "to exalt";
improperare, "to curse"; terms of veneration, such as *benedicti*,
beatissimi, *papa*; and Biblical expressions, like *confortavi eum
dicens* (instead of *his verbis*), *pax tecum* (as a form of salutation).

Christian Latin made its first appearance in literature proper
with Tertullian. No longer are we dealing with anonymous
translators or simple Christians without literary pretensions, but
with writers who have attended the schools and studied rhetoric
and wish to put their education at the service of the new faith.
Tertullian used to be represented as the creator of Christian
Latin, but in fact he found ready to hand a Christian idiom with
a new vocabulary, as we have just shown. As opposed to
Minucius Felix, he used this store liberally, so that we meet
scattered throughout his works Christian neologisms and
elements borrowed from the vulgar tongue alongside of elements
of the literary language. Some neologisms, indeed, can be
attributed to his own making, the most important being *Trinitas*[3]
in its theological sense, to translate Τριάς, which had been used
for the first time by Theophilus of Antioch at the end of the
second century.

His Christian vocabulary was not yet firmly established: so he
denotes baptism both by the Greek terms *baptismus*, *baptisma*,
and by the Latin equivalents *tinctio*, *intinctio*, not to mention
lavacrum, *aqua*, which were moreover used in the centuries that
followed to express the idea of purification contained in that of
baptism; *probole* and its equivalent *prolatio* both express the
notion of bringing forth, production, procession, though it is
true that the first, the Greek, term seems rather to be part of a
quotation.

Many of his expressions are borrowed from the language
of the law: for example, *sequestrare*, "to set apart for safe-
keeping", when speaking of the body deposited in the earth to
wait for the resurrection; *rato habere*, "to find deserving".
Others belong to military language, the Christian's battle against

---

[3] In the treatise *Against Praxeas*, written soon after 213; edited by Ernest
Evans (London, S.P.C.K., 1948).

the world being a traditional, Pauline image: for example, *castra ecclesiae* to denote the service of God; *tirocinium* for "the catechumenate"; and many expressions describing martyrdom as a fight, in using which he was only developing, as often, a natural Christian image.

These metaphorical expressions crowded into his mind in such profusion that the same word suggests several different meanings at once: *statio* is not only, as it is in the *Shepherd* of Hermas, the gathering of Christians, the vigil with its fast, but also the gathering at which one stands ready and on guard to repel the attacks of the devil; *persona* not only means the second Person of the Trinity but also the face, the "mask", through which the Father makes himself heard (*Adv. Prax.*, 14); as for the word *sacramentum*, it is in Tertullian that it began to acquire the various senses that made it one of the words most charged with meaning in all the Christian vocabulary.

But despite all this, Tertullian cannot be considered as beginning a tradition of Christian Latin literature, for there was something that discouraged imitators in his violent originality, which produced a forced Latinity full of striking and unexpected metaphors. St Cyprian on the other hand can more properly be thought of as the first Christian classic. Many of his expressions became common literary coin; the nobility and gravity of his style is found again in pontifical letters of later centuries, as is also the use of the metrical *clausulae*, or sentence-endings, that he took over from Latin rhetoric. It does not surprise us that he should have reacted against the popular expressions used by the first translators of the Bible, which he only admits into his Latin when they are so far become common usage that he needs to use them to be understood by Christians.

Very few neologisms, therefore, were introduced by St Cyprian; but we can nevertheless note the first use of *acerbatio*, "embitterment"; *arcessitio*, "the summons to God, death"; *praefiguratio*, "prefiguration, symbolic image"; and a dozen or so others. The most important of the old words used with new meanings are terms connected with the persecution, such as *confessor*, "confessor of the faith" (more often than in

Tertullian); *lapsi*, "the lapsed, those who have apostatized"; *sacrificati*, "those who have sacrificed to pagan gods"; *libellatici* (neologism), "those who have paid to receive a certificate falsely attesting their willingness to sacrifice". One of the liturgical formulas, *sursum corda, habemus ad Dominum,* already appears in his *De dominica oratione*, ch. 31. His ecclesiastical vocabulary proper is more regular than that of Tertullian; he always refers to baptism by the term *baptisma* (*baptismus*), for example, and keeps the term *tinctio* for the baptism administered by heretics.

Finally it must be remembered that the Latin of the African versions of the Bible seems at the time of St Cyprian to have become established, for his quotations, apart from a few variants probably due to faulty memory, are consistently uniform. We cannot here deal with the Roman correspondents of St Cyprian, who wrote in a much more popular, everyday language (for example, *propter* followed by the ablative, *Ep.*, 22).

The *De Trinitate* of Novatian (mid-third century: ed. W. Yorke Fausset, Cambridge, 1909) is the first original literary work published in Rome. It is written in a clear Latin of a moderate purism, admitting those Graecisms which were part of Christian Latin but adding no new ones: thus the word *dispositio* is always used by Novatian in the sense in which Tertullian had used it alongside of *oeconomia*, to denote the divine plan of salvation, the "economy" of the Trinity. He seems to have introduced no more neologisms than St Cyprian: for example, we can quote *incarnatus, praedestinatio*. He avoids the word *Trinitas*, less from purist motives than from a desire to escape being accused of tritheism; and whilst Tertullian used *Ratio, Sermo,* for the second Person of the Trinity, he uses *Sermo* and *Verbum*, *Verbum* being the most common in the Italian versions of the New Testament. The few letters of Pope Cornelius (251–3) that have come down to us show that at this time the Latin of Christian writers was becoming more uniform. In Africa as in Rome the terminology of church organization and the hierarchy is definitively established, and words like *clerus, episcopus, presbyter, presbyterium,* are henceforth part of normal Christian usage.

In the succeeding generation, Lactantius also is an important witness in our present enquiry. He has been held to be the most Ciceronian of the early Fathers, and his anxiety to avoid vulgarisms is quite evident. Sometimes he affects a philosophical style: *philosophi nostrae sectae*, he calls (*De opifico Dei*, 1, 2) the doctors of the Church; and when he uses the Christian word *adversarius* of the devil, he prefaces it with the more emphatic *ille colluctator et adversarius noster* (*ibid.*, 1, 7). But if we find in his writings a number of Christian neologisms that he had to use to be understood, that is because those terms were no longer regarded as vulgar or everyday, particularly since their use in the Scriptures had given them not simply respectability but even some distinction: so, for example, we find *ambulare* in the sense of "walk (in the right way)"; *lavacrum*, which he raises in tone and meaning by adding *spiritalis* (*Divinarum institutionum libri VII*, 7, 5, 22). Nor does Lactantius seem any less willing to use traditional borrowings from Greek. As for syntax, he could not, despite his purism, avoid using some novel forms, such as the instrumental *in*: *in nomine magistri Dei* (*Inst.*, 4, 15, 2); the infinitive of purpose; and—more surprisingly—a few noun clauses introduced by *quod, quia*. Towards the end of the fourth century, then, Christian Latin tended, as we have said, to become a sort of common language.

FROM THE FOURTH CENTURY TO THE BARBARIAN INVASIONS

From that time the rate of the evolution of the language decreased, but we still cannot properly speak of an established and uniform Christian language. True, there are a common vocabulary, which is further enriched as time goes on, and common syntactical forms; but so far as each author is original he has nevertheless his own language. Even within the *corpus* of the works of each of the great writers differences can be seen. The sermons St Jerome delivered to his monks in Bethlehem are of a freer Latinity than his other writings, and his vocabulary as a translator is more restricted than it is in his letters, for example. St Augustine, immediately after his conversion, wrote some philosophical treatises in a language more or less that of the pagan schools of rhetoric: his sermons, on the other hand, are in a more everyday Latin in which he freely uses vulgarisms; this he does not do in his great theological works, where he uses a purely Christian vocabulary but writes literary Latin. Moreover, it must be said that the language is not equally pure in all Christian authors. If some writers, especially the writers of sermons,[4] express themselves relatively correctly, others either scorn this correctness or cannot rise to the level of literary Latin. Lucifer, Bishop of Cagliari, is a characteristic example of this in the fourth century, and Fulgentius, the author of the *De aetatibus mundi,* is another in the fifth; more and more is this true as the Merovingian age approaches.

But with these reservations we can consider the fourth and fifth centuries as the classical age of Christian Latin. Writers like St Jerome, St Ambrose, St Hilary of Poitiers, St Augustine, and St Leo in the following century, to name only the most important, were read and imitated throughout the Middle Ages. We must now notice a few particular features of the language of the poets, and the neologisms introduced in translations or adaptations from Greek theology. The language of the liturgy deserves a chapter to itself.

In ancient times much more than nowadays poets contrived to speak a different language from that of prose writers. Nor was this only a matter of style: even their grammar and vocabulary were different. This is well enough when the poets are genuinely inspired to poetry, when we are concerned with Virgil or Lucan or passages in Lucretius or Propertius, or with such fine artists as Horace; but with regard to the great bulk of Latin poetry the impression is given of a cold, unnatural art, the more so because its rules were hardly ever overhauled and changed. The first Christian poets inherited these ways of thought and writing. They thought they would be honouring the new faith if they decked it out with these outmoded ornaments. It is no longer a matter, as with the prose authors, of a "baptized"

[4] Such as Laurentius, Maximus of Turin, Petrus Chrysologus, etc.

Latin, but of Christian thought disguised under a pagan chlamys. Let us see what becomes of the simplicity of the Scriptures. Jesus said that one should forgive one's brother "seven times in a day" (Luke 17. 4), or "seventy times seven" (Matt. 18. 22); Juvencus (*Carm.*, 3, 435/6) adapts it in this way:

> *Christus prosequitur: non septem crimina tantum,*
> *sed decuplata super donentur vulnera fratri.*

"Jesus goes on: you must pardon not seven only, but ten times more the wrongs of your brother."

So there is pretence of solemnity, and the Christian vocabulary is avoided: there is nothing Christian about words like *crimina, vulnera*. We are back with the hesitations of Minucius Felix and Lactantius. Juvencus, again, says *Spiramen Sanctum* instead of *Spiritus Sanctus*; instead of *serpens* for the devil we find *anguis* in Prudentius, Orientius, Victorinus Petavionensis, and Paulinus Petricordiae; *nuntius* is used for *angelus* in Prudentius and Commodianus (as in Lactantius and Minucius Felix); *barathrum* for *inferi* in Prudentius and Juvencus; *letifer* for *mortalis*, "causing the death of the soul", in Paulinus of Nola; *balantes* for *oves*, "flock", in Juvencus; *herus* for *Dominus* in Prudentius; etc. The epithet *tonans* applied to Jupiter in Ovid becomes a synonym for *Deus* in the Christian poets Prudentius, Paulinus of Nola, Dracontius, Fortunatus and even in some medieval hymns.

To be fair and not over-generalize, poets like Prudentius and Paulinus of Nola, quite apart from their undoubted spiritual and poetic greatness, misused this artificial secularization of vocabulary less than most. One has only to consult the indexes at the back of the editions of these two authors in the C.S.E.L.[5] to see that they made great use of the Christian vocabulary, reacting against the early tendencies of Christian Latin poetry. As for St Ambrose's hymns, which form the type of liturgical hymnody, they are almost free from those pagan terms; but they will be considered with liturgical Latin.

[5] *Corpus Scriptorum Ecclesiasticorum Latinorum*, Vienna; Nos. 61 and 30.

During these two centuries, the fourth and fifth, it was the adaptation and translation of theological and exegetical works from Greek that most enriched the Christian Latin vocabulary. These works occupy a whole row of volumes in the Greek and Latin *Patrologiae* of Migne.[6] Many anonymous translations, of Origen in particular, date from the fourth century. Rufinus' works consist almost entirely of translations, as do in the fifth and sixth centuries those of Boethius, Cassiodorus (or his school), Eustathius, Mercator and Dionysius Exiguus, to name only the most important; and the same movement continues with Ferrandus, Rusticus, and the translations of the Councils. When we speak of St Jerome we think first of his translations of the Scriptures, but he also translated the homilies of Origen, the *De Spiritu Sancto* of Didymus and the Chronicle of Eusebius; his exegetical work is often an adaptation of Origen. In the same way the exegesis of St Ambrose and St Hilary of Poitiers is altogether inspired by and almost a translation from the Greek Fathers. Details would be out of place here, but a few examples can be given of neologisms or new meanings introduced by the controversies over the Trinity and Christological doctrine.

A term such as ἀπόρροια, "emanation", used by the Arians and, earlier, by those who did not admit the equality of nature of the Son and the Father, caused a good deal of uncertainty. Tertullian has *derivatio*, which is also found in the old Latin translation of St Irenaeus and in St Hilary; but the latter also has *fluxus* and *emanatio* (neologism); the translation of St Irenaeus has *defluxio* or *defluitio*; Victorinus (M. Victorinus Afer) uses *effluentia*. Ἔκτασις, "extension", also describes a monarchic view of the procession of the Trinity: St Hilary hesitates between *extensio, dilatatio* and *protensio*. Once the controversies were past this vocabulary disappears, while *processio*, ἐκπόρευσις, to mean procession in the orthodox sense, and neologisms like *consubstantialis, consubstantialitas, consubstantialiter* became standard terms. The Greek terms which appeared in connection with this last idea, *homoiusios* (*similis*

[6] Note that the old Latin translations of Greek writers are in the Greek series.

substantiae) and *homousios* (*eiusdem substantiae*), are hardly used except in strictly technical contexts, and were not regarded as part of what was properly Latin vocabulary.

For the Incarnation, St Hilary once uses *adoptare*: *dum carnis humilitas adoptatur* (*De Trinitate*, 2, 5, 27); but this seems to be a stylistic device, for the usual term in his work and that of later theologians is, to translate ἀναλαμβάνειν, *assumere*, with the derivative noun *assumptio*; in both languages the prefix implies the idea that Christ not only took on himself humanity but that he raised it to himself. This meaning is not in the verb, common enough from Tertullian to St Leo, *suscipere*. In the previous century *incarnatus*, *incarnatio*, had made their appearance; but other terms were then made up when it was necessary to make clear, as against the Arians and the Apollinarians, that Christ had taken on humanity in its entirety, body and soul, and not only the flesh. The orthodox had therefore made the word ἐνανθρώπησις in place of ἐνσάρκωσις, whence the Latin forms *inhumanatio* and *inhumanari* in Mercator, Facundus and Rusticus, and even *humanatio* (*Act. Conc. Oecum.*, ed. Schwartz, 1, 2, p. 42). Here again, once the controversies ended, theology kept the traditional and primitive terms *incarnatio* and *incarnatus*. A neologism of Mercator, *incarnabilis*, did not survive.

The translators of the acts of the Councils of Ephesus (431), Chalcedon (451) and Constantinople (553) risked neologisms such as *fermentatio* (already used by Tertullian, but in a different sense), and *confermentatio*, corresponding to φυρμός, σύμφυρμος, expressing a heretical view of the hypostatic union which confused the divine and human natures of Christ: the terms *unitio* and *adunitio*, ἕνωσις, expressed the orthodox doctrine, and had already been used in the translation of St Irenaeus and the Fathers of the fourth century; *conventio* in this sense did not last. The end of the controversies also saw the last of such terms as *communificare*, which was opposed to *propriificare* and *propriificatio*, as translations of κοινοποιεῖν and οἰκειοποιεῖν, οἰκείωσις, to express what later theologians called the "communication of idioms", that is, the attribution simply and together to Christ of properties which belong exclusively, in either case, to his divine nature or to his humanity. Without going into details, let us simply say that the establishment of this theological vocabulary can best be seen and studied in the sermons and especially the letters of St Leo.

To signify the Mother of God, the Greek loan-word *theotocos* only appears incidentally in learned discussions, as opposed, for example, to *Christotocos*; from the fourth century onwards the Latin expression *Dei genetrix* prevailed. The compound *Deipara* is only rarely found.

Outside the specially theological field we may mention some experimental translations of Greek terms, such as *deiloquus* (θεολόγος), "theologian"; *deoamabilis* (θεοφιλής) "dear to God"; *deodecenter* (θεοπρεπῶς), "in a manner fitting to the divinity"; etc.; but these are no more than lexicographical curiosities. The Greek loan-words of monastic literature, *eremus, monasterium, coenobium*, and their derivatives, date from this time, as do the compounds *cenodoxia, cenodoxus*, "vainglory, vainglorious". Outside theology altogether, new logical terms or terms used in new senses were created by Victorinus and especially by Boethius, the translators of the logical works of Porphyry and Aristotle; and by Chalcidius, the translator of the *Timaeus*, not to mention Cassiodorus (*De artibus*). These are the beginnings of the terminology of scholastic philosophy and are its basis: we may quote the neuter *accidens* (τὸ συμβεβηκός), "accident", used already by Seneca but now forming various new combinations, *accidens separabile, accidens inseparabile, secundum accidens* and *per accidens*, "accidentally"; other neuters like *adiunctum*, "what is not essential, added, accessory"; *subiectum, obiectum* and *proprium*; new words like *alteritas*, "otherness"; *carentia*, "lack"; *convertentia* for *conversio*, "conversion (of a proposition)"; *particularitas* as opposed to *universalitas*; *praedicamentum*, "predicate, category" (already in St Augustine); *univocus* (συνώνυμος), "having the same name and definition", and its derivatives *univocatio* and *univoce*. Faced with this almost medieval vocabulary we seem to be far not only from classical Latin but even from the normal, traditional Christian Latin.

THE MIDDLE AGES

When, we may wonder, do we date the beginning of the Middle Ages? It is plain that in the Merovingian Age Latin survived, still regarded by those who wrote it (with some Anglo-Saxon exceptions) as their mother tongue, although the language spoken around them was growing ever further from it. The *lingua romana rustica* referred to by the Council of Tours in 813, which was to become the language of preaching, was not considered two centuries earlier as a new language but rather as a country dialect. It was not to be so in the centuries following the Carolingian renaissance: Latin was then studied in the schools and the Romance languages came into their own as languages in their own right.

The development was not the same in all the countries of the west. It is clear that in Italy, and to a lesser degree also in Spain, Latin changed less rapidly: it was at home there, in its own original province, and the schools survived much longer. If we read, for example, the collections of pontifical letters, such as that of Gundlach,[7] we can hardly say where we ought to draw a dividing line, for we are faced with a more or less uniform and continuous linguistic tradition. The study of the letters of Cassiodorus († *c.* 580), who had been the minister of the Gothic king Theodoric before he retired to found his monastery, in which his monks should work to continue the patristic tradition, shows us a civilization still very much alive, in a prose which has not lost its Roman gravity. The outlook is blacker when we come to Gregory the Great († 604), but still in his writings Latin has not yet lost its firmness. In Spain, Martin of Braga († 579) and later, Isidore of Seville († 636), bear witness to the continued knowledge of Latin, not yet overwhelmed by the tides of barbarism.

Things were different in the lands which made up the ancient Gaul. Immediately after the invasions, names like those of Salvian of Marseilles († *c.* 490) and Sidonius Apollinaris

---

[7] In *Monumenta Germaniae Historiae, Epistolae III: Epistolae Merovingici et Karolini Aevi*, t. 1 (Berlin, 1892).

(† 498) prove that the literary tradition was kept alive for some time. But from the sixth century onwards the schools gradually disappeared, and a poet like Fortunatus (who was born in Italy) shows up as a rare survival. The prose (if not the poetry) of St Avitus, and even more that of Gregory of Tours, was strongly influenced by the popular tongue; its morphology as well as its syntax had been barbarized. In the Gothic Psalter, *oves* is written *obes*, and conversely *civis resumtis* in the Gothic Breviary means *cibis resumptis*. An introit in the Gallican Liturgy is called *antiphona ad praelegendo*, instead of *ad praelegendum*— the final *m* has dropped off.

A few monastic centres continued copying the writings of the Fathers and even of profane authors, but original works of theology or exegesis were no longer being written. Only hagiographic and liturgical literature remained living, the latter including some works worthy of our consideration later. As for the lives of the saints, they were written in a Latin less barbarous than that of the charters of this period, in so far, that is, as the manuscript tradition has not corrected their orthography. In the country districts, on the other hand, the ignorance of the clergy had become very great by the end of the Merovingian period: St Boniface, who came from Wessex and died as Bishop of Mainz in 754, tells of a Frankish priest who baptized with these words: *baptizo te in nomine Patria et Filia et Spiritus Sancti*!

It was this ignorance against which Charlemagne and his counsellors took action. The "renaissance" which then took place had been prepared for by the work of the monastic teachers who came from Ireland (then called *Scoti*) and by the reforms of Pepin the Short. Driven by Charlemagne and his famous cartulary *De scolis*, which was followed by others, clerics returned to the study of grammar and rhetoric. At first these were taught by foreign teachers sent for by the king, the Anglo-Saxon Alcuin of York and Paulus Diaconus from Lombardy, but in the following century and after the foremost authors are Franks: Walafrid Strabo, Amalarius of Lyons, Lupus of Ferrières and many others. But we must guard against a false impression that may be given by the use of the word "renaissance". True, the letters of a man like Lupus of Ferrières deal with the concerns of a humanist, but in general this is not a return to antiquity as the Renaissance was to be later. Its aims were much more modest: the better understanding of the Scriptures, and the formation of a clergy able to "know the law of God and preach it to the people". It was thus essentially a renaissance of the Latin of the Church.

And this is true of the six centuries that followed. It is impossible to give a picture of Christian Latin down to the fifteenth century in a few pages; literary historians like Max Manitius[8] and Joseph de Ghellinck[9] have laboured to set out the story of the development of this vast literature. We shall content ourselves with a few remarks about the grammar and, especially, the vocabulary of this period. As we have just suggested, the writers of the Middle Ages, as opposed to those of six centuries later, were quite without any preconceived notions of classical Latinity. If some turn of phrase was not Ciceronian but only to be found in Biblical or patristic Latin, they used it without any hesitation, implicitly recognizing the existence of a language which was properly speaking Christian. Smaragdus of St Michael and Gottschalk of Orbais had already formulated this principle in the ninth century. Some modern scholars, having only a classical background, have thought to discover in some medieval authors this or that innovation, when really it is simply a matter of a usage already attested from the time of the Fathers. It is wrong to speak of medieval syntax in ecclesiastical writers, unless the beginning of the Middle Ages can be pushed back to the end of the third century.

Thus a consecutive clause with an indicative verb introduced by *quod* is, according to some linguists, from vulgar Latin. But Thomas of Celano, in the thirteenth century, had not been taught vulgar Latin; if he writes a sentence like this: *tanto*

[8] *Geschichte der lateinischen Literatur des Mittelalters*, vol. 1, 1911; vol. 2, 1923; vol. 3, 1931; being vol. IX, 2, of *Handbuch der klassischen Altertumswissenschaft*, Munich.

[9] *Patristique et Moyen Age*, 3 vols., Gembloux, 1946–8; and *Littérature latine au moyen âge*, 2 vols., Bloud et Gay, 1939.

dolore afficior, quod vix possum aliud cogitare, "I am affected
by such feeling that I can scarcely think of anything else"
(*Vita Francisci,* 1, 46, 14), it was because he had met such
constructions in the works of the Fathers; and indeed this *quod*
is widely attested in the patristic period. An expression like *ad
propria reverti* or *remeare,* "to go home", seems really medieval,
but it is to be found already in St Augustine and the letters of
Pope Gelasius. Not to give too many examples, when we read
dic mihi qualis est ista puella (*Gesta Romanorum* 5, ed. Oesterley) [10]
we seem to hear a Frenchman speaking Latin, and yet this
qualis in the sense of *quis* is attested often in the works of St
Augustine.

On the other hand phrases like *ludere ad talos,* "to play at
dice", and *uno die,* "one day", betray the influence which the
vernaculars had in increasing measure on medieval Latin.
Even after the Renaissance a German or an Englishman did not
write Latin like a Frenchman or an Italian; good Latinists who
did not betray their origin were rare.

These remarks concern only properly ecclesiastical writers
and those who were consciously maintaining a tradition. But
apart from their works, there is in medieval Latin a whole mass
of writings which are almost without interest for the philologist,
if not for the historian. And this is most true when we are
dealing with vocabulary. If we look through the full volumes of
the *Glossarium* of du Cange, which moreover is incomplete and
does not cover, for example, philosophical writings, we are dis-
mayed by the monstrous proliferation of words. It is true that
we find there a certain number of neologisms formed with the
traditional prefixes and suffixes, such that it seems that those
words must have first appeared much earlier: for example,
fungibilis, fungibilitas, illegitimitas and many others with a
similarly authentic Latin air. But on the other hand we leave
respectable Latin behind when we come upon words ending in
-antia instead of *-atio* (*venerantia*), in *-agium* instead of *-aticum,*
etc. At the same time there was a great invasion of German,

[10] A collection of stories made in the thirteenth century for the use of
preachers.

English, French, Italian and Spanish words, dressed up with a Latin ending. Relations with the east and Constantinople even introduced some Greek words, such as *exas*, the number six, *exafoti*, a six-branched candlestick; and a few Arabic words like *amiras, amireus, admiraldus*, from which comes our *admiral*, and so on. But, we must repeat, Christian Latin in general escaped this corruption. We find no barbaric neologisms in liturgical or devotional writers, nor in the theologians, except so far as they allowed themselves to be swamped by the scholastic jargon. But against this, in letters, in hagiography, in canon law, writers used more new words, but only when they needed to signify contemporary objects, offices or institutions: for example, *ballivus*, "bailiff", *marca*, "mark", *placitum*, "plea", etc.

Separate notice must be taken of the enriching of the philosophical vocabulary by the Scholastics. Alongside of old words used in new senses, like *agens*, "agent", *intellectus agens*, "the active intellect", there appeared a host of new terms, such as *aequivalentia* and *aequivalentum*, "equivalence"; *aequivalens*, "equivalent"; *aeviternitas*, the eternity shared in by the creation as opposed to *aeternitas*, the divine eternity; *agibilis*, "feasible"; *agibilitas*, "feasibility"; *alietas*, "otherness"; *quidditas*, formed from *quid* as *qualitas, quantitas*, from *qualis, quantus*, "whatness, the essence of a thing"; *alternalis*, "converse"; *appetibilitas*, "desirability"; etc. In the last two centuries of the Middle Ages the Latin of the theologians was to be contaminated by this new terminology.

To this new and almost barbarous Latin the writers of secular works preferred the Latinity of the good authors of the twelfth and thirteenth centuries. Leaving aside the poets, who were generally too preoccupied with their classical models to be original, and the writers of hymns and sequences, of whom we shall speak in a moment, this means writers like St Bernard of Clairvaux, Peter of Blois, St Bonaventure and many others, who—and especially the first—best realized in their own style the ideal of medieval Latin. The Roman prose-writers never lost a certain flavour of artifice and conscious culture; but these give us the impression of greater simplicity which yet does not lack distinction: it is a language which flows naturally, with neither pretensions nor narrow restraint, free from the worries of the purist. Their Latin sounds like their mother tongue, natural to them, which they use as rightly theirs, with a pleasing freedom. We can admire Cicero's prose; but it is almost a pleasant relaxation to turn from it to the writings of St Bernard.

MODERN TIMES

What was left of this freedom after the Renaissance and the return to classical standards? First of all we must be careful not to make too absolute a division; just as in the twelfth and thirteenth centuries we find poets overfond of imitating classical models, so we find that in the sixteenth there are still writers who use Latin with an easy familiarity. But so far as concerns the Latin literature of the Church it can nevertheless be said that the patristic and medieval tradition was broken. This break can actually be seen happening in the humanist reform of the hymns of the Roman breviary, which was first tried out in the sixteenth century and achieved in the seventeenth. Even today there are arguments as to whether it was fitting that these hymns should be revised by four Jesuits at the order of Urban VIII to make them conform more closely to the classical rules of grammar and prosody, and some scholars deplore that the real beauty of the old Christian language and respect for it should have been sacrificed for a few slight improvements. Somewhere I read a eulogy of the good Latinity of St Alphonsus Liguori: it was compared with Seneca's, but not with that of St Bernard or St Augustine.

Here is an example from our own times. The success of the new translation of the Psalms, which recalls the Latin of the humanists rather than that of the Fathers or of the Vulgate, shows that our contemporary clergy, who have for the most part been taught classical Latin, are more at home with this version and have lost the feeling for Christian Latin. And it also shows that Church circles in Rome continue in the humanist

tradition, and that if the study of the Latin of the Fathers and
of the Bible is commended and honoured in scholarly circles
(and that at Rome too), in monasteries and in the more important seminaries, yet in the Church as a whole the knowledge
of Christian Latin is declining. In any case, no one would now
try to write in that kind of Latin. But is it not equally artificial
for a twentieth-century European to write in a Latin more or
less classical?

Whatever the answer to the problem of the survival of Latin
in the Church, the fact is that for four centuries it has no longer
been written according to the syntax of St Augustine; that now
belongs to the past—a past which is venerable and now the
object of much careful study, but the past nevertheless. On the
other hand, what has remained living in the Church is the
Christian vocabulary, in so far as it is necessary to keep
traditional terms and to make new ones for contemporary
needs. There is thus a technical jargon of theology: convincing
evidence of this can be found in the manuals, or in those
original writings still produced in Latin. There are also the
pontifical documents, and the technical language of canon law;
just as all lawyers have their jargon, canon lawyers speak, with
regard to marriage, of *impedimenta dirimentia*, "diriment
impediments", and of *sanatio in radice*, "regularization of
marriage with a retro-active effect". New terms have had to be
made, such as *benedictio telegraphi*. We could listen *Marconica
ope* (Pius XI, October 14th, 1934), "thanks to Marconi", thanks
to radio. It is artificial, but necessary, just as are all the terms
denoting functions in the Roman curia.

But a language which seems to have enjoyed a revival of
interest with a wider public[11] and which has remained more
alive in our minds is that of the liturgy. Will that Latin give
place to the various modern vernaculars? Will there be, in the
centuries to come, an English, and a French, liturgy, as there is
a Slavonic or Greek liturgy now? To restrict ourselves simply to

[11] As proof of this we could cite, besides the many English-Latin Missals,
such a work as Mary Perkins, *Your Catholic Language*, London and
New York, Sheed and Ward, 1942.

the task in hand, let us state two facts: during the first centuries of Christianity the Latin of the services was for the congregation a living language, whereas now between the congregation and the celebrant a screen is set up which only a small minority can pierce; on the other hand, would not the liturgy lose its sacred character if the services and prayers of the Church were in a familiar and everyday language? Whatever the answer, if there is still a living Christian Latin, it is that of the liturgy: the mother tongue which in its prayers and hymns cradled our infancy in the faith, a living language, not in the ordinary and material sense that it produces new works and creates new words, but spiritually, in our hearts, able more than any other Latin to move the spirits of those who hear it.

CHAPTER XIV

LITURGICAL LATIN

The historians of the liturgy also have their technical terms, to denote the objects used in worship, vestments, rites and details of buildings: so *corporalis palla*, "corporal"; *casula, planeta*, "chasuble"; *commixtio*, the mixing of a portion of the conse-created host in the chalice; *absis, absida*, "choir, apse"; etc. But by "liturgical Latin" we mean here the language of the services and the administration of the sacraments as it is today contained in the Missal, Breviary, Pontifical and Ritual; and we restrict ourselves for our quotations to the two first named, as sufficient to characterize this language.

After the liturgy had been established in its broad outlines as it has since been preserved, that is since the beginning of the Middle Ages, a large number of different collections appeared. First the Sacramentaries, which contain the prayers of the Mass and the formularies for benedictions (of fonts, etc.) and for consecrations: the Leonine, the definitive form of which prob-ably dates from the end of the sixth century; the Gelasian (seventh, eighth centuries); the Gregorian, the definitive text of which is of the tenth century. These are the main ones; they depend one from another and partly contain the same texts. Most of the prayers in the present Missal go back to them. There were others, such as the Gallican Missal (or Sacra-mentary) of Merovingian times; the Mozarabic Missal, used in Visigothic Spain; and the Ambrosian Missal of Milan. The *Ordines Romani*, the oldest of which go back to the eighth century, contain directions for the ritual of different ceremonies; from them comes the *Ceremonial of Bishops*. There were also the Graduals, containing the chants for the Mass; the Antiphonaries, for the anthems, especially for Vespers; Lectionaries, collections of Epistles; Evangelaries, Psalters, Hymnaries, Martyrologies, etc.[1]

Returning to the Latin of the Missal and the Breviary, it should first be noted that there is no uniformity of language: there we may find the Latin of the Fathers and the Bible; a Latin more specifically liturgical, of the collects and prefaces; and lastly that of the hymns and sequences. Many of the lessons of the Breviary are actually from patristic Latin, homilies or sermons (and sometimes treatises) of St Cyprian, St Augustine, St Ambrose, St Jerome, St Leo, St Gregory, and a few translations from the Greek Fathers, like St John Chrysostom; other lessons are taken from medieval authors such as St Bernard; lastly, there are some of more recent composition, when they deal with the life of a saint, or sometimes when they give a part of a commentary on the Gospel in the third nocturn: these exist from all periods, according as feasts of saints were established in the Latin Church. What we say about Christian Latin in general will also apply to these different texts.

BIBLICAL LATIN IN THE LITURGY

There is a good deal of Biblical Latin in the liturgy; it was, after all, its original foundation: psalms, epistles, the Gospels, anthems and lessons taken from the books of the Old and New Testaments. St Jerome translated from the Hebrew (or the Aramaic) all the "protocanonical" books of the Old Testament. As for the "deuterocanonical" ones—those which are not found in the Jewish but only in the Greek Bible (1 and 2 Machabees, Tobias, Judith, Wisdom, Ecclesiasticus and Baruch)—these he did not touch, with the exception of Judith and Tobias, which he revised (rather than translated) from a "Chaldaean", that is, Aramaic, text. In the New Testament, he certainly revised the Gospels with the Greek text, but there is some doubt whether he revised the rest.

[1] See relevant volumes in section X of this series, "The Worship of the Church".

10—s.l.

Clearly whoever wishes to study the Vulgate Old Testament from the exegetical point of view needs to know Hebrew. But we are only concerned with the Latinity of this translation and can only remark in passing on two things: it is not in Jerome's normal style, nor did the Vulgate make Christian Latin. As we have explained above, it had already been made by the first translations of the Bible and by the writings of the Fathers of the third and fourth centuries. But even without the Hebrew it is possible to feel, in this translation-Latin, the foreignness, for example, of the lyrical quality of the prophets, as in this passage from Isaias (60. 1 and 6) which is read as the Epistle for the Epiphany: *Surge, illuminare, Jerusalem; quia venit lumen tuum et gloria Domini super te orta est*: "Arise, be enlightened, O Jerusalem: for thy light is come, and the glory of the Lord is risen upon thee." Or this eastern picture: *Inundatio camelorum operiet te, dromadarii Madian et Epha; omnes de Saba venient, aurum et thus deferentes, laudem Domini annuntiantes*: "The multitude of camels shall cover thee, the dromedaries of Madian and Epha: all they from Saba shall come, bringing gold and frankincense and showing forth praise to the Lord."[2] But there is no need to multiply examples and observations of this kind, which are in any case more literary than linguistic.

The Latin of the New Testament is simpler, at least in the Gospels and Acts. This is not vulgar Latin, but rather a Latin used every day, conforming to normal usage but influenced also by certain Greek constructions. It is by reading this Latin that anyone wishing to begin on Christian Latin should start. As for the Epistles of St Paul, their difficulty lies not in the Latin but in the thought of the Apostle, which is not always easy to grasp; the same difficulty is there in the Greek, which is strained to express his meaning.

Of the Latin of the Bible, that of the Psalms has played the most important part in the formation of the liturgy. Not only are they to be found in all the Breviary offices but scattered throughout the whole liturgy—introits, graduals, the beginning of the Mass, certain parts of the Offertory recited by the priest,

[2] Translations from Douay version.

and certain sung parts of the Offertory and the Communion, where the text is sometimes different from that of the Vulgate. For St Jerome made several revisions of the translation of the Psalms: since the faithful already had a Latin version with which they were familiar, he tried first to correct that version, without altering too much, from the Greek of the Septuagint (this is probably the so-called "Roman" psalter); then, to get closer to the Hebrew, he took up again his work on the Septuagint, with the help of Origen's *Hexapla*, one of the columns of which gave the Hebrew text; and this is the "Gallican" psalter; but it is not the last: having undertaken to translate the whole of the Old Testament from the Hebrew, St Jerome made a third version of the Psalms *secundum veritatem hebraicam*. But whereas his translation of the rest was accepted and spread without much difficulty, so that in the seventh century its victory over other versions was more or less accomplished, his translation of the psalter met with more opposition. It would no doubt ultimately have triumphed had not the authority of Alcuin ensured the success of Jerome's second revision, the Gallican psalter. It is thus the latter which is now to be found in the Vulgate.

Let us pause for a moment on this Vulgate text of the Psalms; despite its imperfections, it is evidence of venerable antiquity. It is in a less correct Latin, quite unlike that of the rest of the Bible, conserving traces of the older versions. We must be careful not to exaggerate difficulties nor to decide too quickly that this or that construction is untranslatable: there are only a few such passages, where the translator did not understand and was content to render his original by an approximately word for word version. In these cases, scholars are agreed that we have a transcription of an already faulty Septuagint text. So it happens that the philological explanation of a verse has to go beyond Latin linguistics. For example:

Ps. 48. 7-9: *Qui confidunt in virtute sua, et in multitudine divitiarum suarum gloriantur.*

Frater non redimit, redimet homo, non dabit Deo placationem suam.

Et pretium redemptionis animae suae, et laborabit in aeternum, et vivet adhuc in finem.

The Hebrew says: "They trust in their wealth, and boast of the abundance of their riches.

"Man cannot at all give ransom, cannot give to Yahweh his price.

"For indeed, the ransom of life is too costly, and he must give up for ever (*sc.* the hope of paying it)."

And here is a word for word translation of the Latin:

"They trust in their own power, and boast of the abundance of their riches.

"A brother does not ransom, man will ransom, he will not give to God his satisfaction.

"Or the price of the redemption of his soul, and he will labour to eternity, and will live still to the end."

It is impossible to see the connection of ideas in the last two verses. And here is another example of bizarre Latin:

Ps. 109. 7: . . . *conquassabit capita in terra multorum.*

The Hebrew says: "He doth smite chiefs, going over a wide land." (The Greek of the Septuagint, like the Vulgate, has a future: "he will smite".)

Two translations of the Latin are possible: "He will break the heads of many to the ground" (with an odd order of words); "in the lands of many (i.e. far and wide)"; neither is satisfactory.

We repeat, such hopeless passages are exceptions. It is more important to notice the traces of Hebrew style still to be perceived in our text of the Psalms. For example, there are the feminines used instead of the neuter: *Unam petii a Domino, hanc requiram* (Ps. 26. 4): "One request I have ever made of the Lord, let me claim it still." There are genitives equivalent to an adjective, which was to become a stylistic habit in Christian Latin: *viri sanguinum* (Ps. 25. 9): "the blood-thirsty"; *virga directionis* (Ps. 44. 7): "sceptre of thy royalty"; abstract nouns are used as predicates of verbs usually construed with concrete objects: *amictus lumine* (Ps. 103. 2): "The light is a garment thou dost wrap about thee." Despite its strangeness and even its awkwardness the Latin of the Psalms is nevertheless capable of making us feel the sublimity of the poetry of the Bible. There is, for example, the grandeur of the evocation of aspects of nature filled with the divine Presence: *qui dat nivem sicut lanam, nebulam sicut cinerem spargit* (Ps. 147. 6): "Now he spreads a pall of snow, covers earth with an ashy veil of rime." Nature is made living before the manifestation of God: *montes exsulta- verunt ut arietes, et colles sicut agni ovium* (Ps. 113. 4): "Up leapt, like rams, the startled mountains, up leapt the hills, like yearling sheep." The Lord appeared: *inclinavit caelos et des- cendit, et caligo sub pedibus eius; et ascendit super cherubim et volavit* (Ps. 17. 10–11): "He bade heaven stoop, and came down to earth, with a dark cloud at his feet; he came, cherub-mounted, borne up on the wings of the wind." And the psalmist expresses with striking images the majesty of the universal presence of the divinity: *si ascendero in caelum, tu illic es; si descendero in infernum, ades* (Ps. 138. 8): "If I should climb up to heaven, thou art there; if I sink down to the world beneath, thou art present still." At every moment the Psalms break into passionate and enthusiastic bursts of praise, with the imperatives: *laudate, exsultate, confitemini, annuntiate, jubilate*; or of supplication: *miserere mei, Domine*; or of hope: *in te, Domine, speravi*. This is why the Church, inheriting the Psalms from the Jews, has made from them one of the most regular forms of prayer in the liturgy. Outside of Biblical texts, the Latin used in the liturgy itself is that of invocations, prefaces and prayers, and that of hymns and sequences.

LITURGICAL PRAYERS AND PREFACES

It is true, however, that the invocations and acclamations of the liturgy are generally themselves taken from the Bible. *Amen, alleluia, hosanna*, are Hebrew terms; *pax vobis, Dominus vobiscum*, are Biblical forms of salutation and of Jewish origin, as also is the solemn expression: "God of Abraham, Isaac and Jacob." The *sanctus* is taken from Isaias (6. 3): *et clamabant alter ad alterum et dicebant: sanctus, sanctus, sanctus Dominus Deus exercitum; plena est omnis terra gloria eius*: "And ever the

same cry passed between them, Holy, holy, holy is the Lord
God of hosts; all the earth is full of his glory." The *dignus est*
is taken from a verse of the Apocalypse (5. 12); the *agnus Dei* is
the salutation of John the Baptist to Jesus: *ecce agnus Dei, ecce
qui tollit peccatum mundi* (John 1. 29); the *Domine non sum
dignus* is the centurion's prayer (Matt. 8. 8). The Greek invocation, *kyrie eleison*, "Lord have mercy", has been retained in
the Latin liturgy since its formation, and is also from the
Bible: ἐλέησόν με, *miserere mei*, is common in the Psalms: notice
especially ἐλέησόν με, κύριε, in Ps. 9. 14. Nearer no doubt to the
pagan rhetoric, to the classical rhetoric, are the longer prayers of
a discursive character, such as the eucharistic prayers, the prefaces, the canon and the collects.

The prayers of the Eucharist, the most ancient form of
Christian worship, are represented in our liturgy by the different
prefaces and the prayers of the canon (that is, fixed prayers,
according to a rule). It was in the beginning an improvised
service, and began with a dialogue between the celebrant and
the people, the *sursum corda*, attested, as we have said, as early
as St Cyprian, who uses the word *praefatio* for the preliminary
invitation to pray. The same word is always used for the preface
in the Gregorian Sacramentary, while the Leonine uses the
word *preces*; the Gallican and Mozarabic liturgies also have
illatio, "prayer after the offerings", or *contestatio*, "attestation
of the greatness of God, of the Holy Trinity". The first Sacramentaries preserved a good number of prefaces, whereas only
fourteen are to be found in the Gregorian. The chief characteristic of their style is its priestly solemnity. Following the poetic
tradition of the Psalms and also the rules of classical rhetoric,
they abound in parallelisms and antitheses; but it is not simply
a matter of the embellishments proper to an elevated style, for
these phrases embody the majesty and solemnity of the occasion.
Thus on the feast of Epiphany: *cum Unigenitus tuus in substantia
nostrae mortalitatis apparuit, nova nos in immortalitatis suae
luce reparavit*, "For when thine only-begotten Son showed himself in the substance of our mortal nature, he restored us by the
new light of his own immortality." And as in the visions of the

prophets and the Revelation of St John, we are invited to join the powers of heaven in singing the *Sanctus*.

Besides the Mass prefaces, there are those for the benediction of fonts and others as well: the *Exultet* of the vigil of Easter belongs to this kind of prayer, though it has a more marked poetic colouring and is less restrained in its use of rhetoric.

The Latin canon of the Mass is called *actio* in the Gelasian Sacramentary (from *agere*, to celebrate Mass); but the Gregorian Sacramentary afterwards adopted the word *canon*. Essentially, these prayers go back to the fifth century, but their elements may be found in the *De sacramentis* of St Ambrose: *Dicit sacerdos: fac nobis, inquit, hanc oblationem scriptam, rationabilem, acceptabilem . . .* "The priest says: grant us that this offering be approved, worthy,[3] acceptable . . ." The canon as we now read it in our Missals first appears in the Gelasian, and then in its definitive form in the Gregorian Sacramentary. It has the fullness and majesty of the best Roman prose. According to the rules of traditional rhetoric, this fullness is achieved by piling up synonyms or near-equivalents:

rogamus ac petimus;
quam pacificare, custodire, adunare et regere digneris toto orbe terrarum;
uti accepta habeas et benedicas haec dona, haec munera, haec sancta sacrificia illibata;
hostiam puram, hostiam sanctam, hostiam immaculatam;
per quem haec omnia, Domine, semper bona creas, sanctificas, vivificas, benedicis, et praestas nobis.

This repetition is sometimes reinforced by alliteration: *de tuis donis ac datis*. In the prayer after the elevation, *Unde et memores*, this multiplication of terms contributes to the balance of the whole period, the key word in which is *offerimus*. It also recalls the parallelism of the poetry of the Bible: *panem sanctum vitae aeternae et calicem salutis perpetuae*; in the same way, this ornate style evokes, within the Christian way of thinking,

---

[3] Others translate this word, which corresponds to the Greek λογικός, as "spiritual".

images familiar from the Psalms: *supra quae propitio ac sereno vultu respicere digneris* recalls *illustra faciem tuam super servum tuum* (Ps. 30. 17) or else *illuminet vultum tuum super nos* (Ps. 66. 2). The presence of God is the "sight" of God: *in conspectu divinae majestatis tuae,* as in Ps. 16 and elsewhere: *in conspectu tuo.*

The vocabulary is patristic, more even than biblical, as is shown by such terms as *servitus, servi,* used of priests; *familia tua, plebs tua,* of the faithful; *refrigerium,* of eternal rest; etc. So this solemn prayer of the canon of the Mass is both stamped with the Roman *gravitas* and faithful to the style and vocabulary traditionally Christian.

Although it has not the solemn character of that of the prefaces and the canon, the style of the collects and other prayers nevertheless is very similar. The term *collecta* (once *collectio* in Gaul), which now refers to the first prayer of the Mass after the preparation, meant in primitive times, not to mention its other senses, "the prayer which concludes, which sums up for everybody", from *colligere orationem* (Cassian, *Inst.,* 2, 10 *tit.; Conc. Agath. can.* 30, Mansi 8, *c.* 330). The names of these prayers have varied; for example, in the Gregorian Sacramentary the secret is called *(oratio) super oblata,* "after the offerings", and the postcommunion *(oratio) ad complendum,* "to finish", and is followed by a benediction.

From the fourth to the seventh century the Roman liturgists composed a great number of prayers both of brief simplicity and smooth elegance, and always full of profound meaning.[4] Compilers were concerned, firstly, to be understood by all when they expressed some religious feeling or thought pertaining to the feast being celebrated, and secondly, to avoid familiarity in creating a style especially fitting for prayer and sufficiently priestly and holy to be worthy of the mysteries expressed.

Generally a collect begins with an invocation, *Deus,* or more

[4] The liturgy of the Gallo-Romans and the Spanish, in the prefaces as in the other prayers, presents quite different characteristics: there is more exuberant prolixity, the images are subtler and more mannered. But there are some fine things in it, like the Easter *Exultet,* of such elaborate grace, which has moreover passed into the Roman liturgy.

fully, *Omnipotens sempiterne Deus*. After a relative or comparative clause which sets out the reason for the request, this is
presented with the formulas: *concede, quaesumus, ut . . .*; *da* or
tribue, quaesumus, ut . . .; or more simply the imperative *da*
followed by the infinitive. It sometimes happens that the
request is put first, in the form of an imperative or an optative
subjunctive, as in the postcommunion for the Mass of Christmas at dawn: *huius nos, Domine, sacramenti semper novitas
natalis instauret, cuius nativitas singularis humanum repulit
vetustatem*, "May the new life derived from this sacrament ever
revive us, O Lord: since it is his sacrament, whose wonderful
birth hath overcome the old man." The Gregorian Sacramentary
began thus: *eius nos, Domine, sacramenti semper natalis instauret
. . .*, "May the anniversary of this mystery . . ."; so an antithesis
has been introduced between the words *novitas* and *vetustas* to
stress the ideas of renewal and redemption. These antitheses
are the most common features of the style of these prayers; in
the same Mass, the collect of our Missal and the Gregorian
Sacramentary contrasts faith and works: *ut . . . hoc nostro
resplendeat opere, quod per fidem fulget in mente*, "That we . . .
may show forth in our actions that which by faith shineth in
our minds." The Secret, bringing together Man and God the
Redeemer, also opposes our earthly origin and our heavenly
destiny: *ut, sicut Homo genitus idem refulsit et Deus, sic nobis
haec terrena substantia conferat quod divinum est*, "That even as
he who was born Man shone forth also as God, so may this
earthly substance bestow upon us that which is divine."

Lastly, these prayers gain their air of serious Latin also from
the use of rhythmical *clausulae*. In the classical period prose
writers had sought a balance between long and short syllables,
especially at the end of clauses; it was at that time a matter of
metrical *clausulae*. In patristic times, when the quantities of
syllables were obscured, the ends of clauses were marked rather
by the accent, so that the *clausulae* are better called rhythmical.
Writers who wanted to produce an educated prose used them
and so they passed into the ancient liturgical prayers. The name
of *cursus* was given to these *clausulae*. So there were

distinguished, for example, the *cursus planus*, in which the second and fifth syllables from the end were accented, as in the prayer quoted above: *fúlget in ménte*; the dispondaic *cursus*, with the accent on the second and sixth from the end, as in the preface of Christmas: *amórem rapiámur*; the *cursus velox*, with the accent on the second and seventh, as in *júgiter sentiámus*; the *cursus tardus*, accenting the third and sixth, as in *sub sacraménto mirábili*. This fact must be stressed in order to show that we are, in these liturgical prayers, far from an improvised, unpolished prose; all the devices of rhetoric were pressed into service to make this Latin serious and solemn, worthy to be addressed to God.[5]

HYMNS AND SEQUENCES

The Psalms were sung in the primitive Church, and the invocations we have been considering were doubtless psalmodic. Hymns were not introduced until later. The word itself is Greek and means a song in honour of the Gods, for example, the Homeric Hymns. Among the first Christians it still had this general sense. So for Lactantius David is the writer of the divine hymns, *divinorum scriptor hymnorum* (*Inst.*, 3, 5, 14), while St Jerome distinguished Psalms from hymns, the latter celebrating the greatness and majesty of God in a more solemn manner than the Psalms, which were above all intended for edification (*ad ethicum locum pertinent, Comm. in Ephes.*, III, 5, 19). For St Augustine hymns were simply songs of praise to God, *hymni sunt laudes Dei cum cantico* (*Enarr. in Psal.* 72, 1).

As for metrical hymns, it was St Hilary of Poitiers, and then St Ambrose in Milan, who first had them sung during the services. Ambrosian hymns are made up of iambic dimeters. They rapidly became famous, so famous that any hymns made in this metre came to be called Ambrosian; even the *Te Deum* was called *hymnus ambrosianus*, though this was misusing the

[5] See on the *cursus* of the collects F. Amiot, *History of the Mass*, pp. 44–5, in this series.

term. Of all those which have been attributed to St Ambrose himself, only eight are authentic, or even only four according to certain scholars, and these are still in our Breviary: they are *Aeterne rerum conditor; Deus creator omnium; Veni, redemptor gentium*; and *Jam surgit hora tertia*. They have the merit of being Christian in a manner more original and less trammelled by the tricks of traditional versification, translating a religious thought or prayer in a simple and clear way in a restrained poetic style.

The Breviary also contains hymns from the works of Prudentius (fourth century), Sedulius and Elpis (fifth century). Their verses, while taking note of the accentuation, are still based on scansion according to quantity, the length of the syllables; Auspicius, however, at the end of the fifth century, introduced verses no longer based on classical prosody, but on accentual scansion alone, which became standard medieval practice.

At first the place of hymns in the liturgy was restricted. The council of Braga in 563 forbade them, but seventy years later the council of Toledo made their use obligatory in Spain and France. The Roman liturgy, however, only finally introduced them into its important services about the eleventh or twelfth century. The Rule of St Benedict includes them in all the canonical hours.

There are many medieval hymnaries, or collections of hymns; a book of this sort is mentioned by Gennadius, as early as the end of the fifth century. To give some idea of the numbers of hymns that were written we need only remark that the collection of Dreves-Blume, *Analecta hymnica medii aevi* (Leipzig, 1886–1922), one of the latest published, contains one hundred and fifty volumes. And new feasts have increased that number during the last three hundred years.

Obviously, over such a long period, the Latin of this religious poetry will be of very varying merit. Looking at them all together, we can pick out a good many masterpieces, not only from the best period of the twelfth and thirteenth centuries but even from Merovingian and Carolingian times. These apart, there is a seemingly infinite number of more ordinary pieces, some simple to the point of platitude, others more mannered. But taken all together, they rarely offer us bad Latin. We can only refer here to works specially concerned with this literature.[6] Let us merely say what distinguishes this Christian poetry from the last productions of pagan antiquity which had become an artificial pastime, repeating over and over again without seeming to get tired of them the same mythological allusions, so that, as we have said, it no longer has any interest for us.

The style of the hymns is simpler.[7] Written to say something, they always express some thought or feeling: they formulate a Christian truth, a specific dogma, at the same time as they breathe a fervent prayer. And this is true of all periods. It is as true of the hymns of St Ambrose as of the sequences of St Thomas Aquinas. True, the material is sometimes a bit thin: we are reminded of medieval statues in which the spirit is plainly discernible in the face. Ancient art had been the glorification of the body, of the external form; the hymn was above all spiritual, and we sense its spirit the better since Gregorian plainchant exactly matches the forms of the verse.

Fortunatus was a poet of the Merovingian period. Yet what splendour and nobility there is in the beginning of the hymn *Vexilla regis prodeunt*, its marching rhythm calling up the procession in some cathedral or basilica, with (according to Gregory of Tours) the great crucifix lit by the candles carried before it: *fulget crucis mysterium!* In the same writer's *Pange, lingua*[8] the verse *vagit infans . . .* calls vividly to our minds the Child in the manger wrapped by his mother in swaddling clothes; and what tenderness there is in the following verse, in which the

---

[6] Among others: U. Chevalier, *Bibliothèque liturgique*, tome 1: *Poésie liturgique du moyen âge* (Paris, 1893; the other volumes are collections); F. J. E. Raby, *A History of Christian Latin Poetry from the Beginnings to the Close of the Middle Ages* (Oxford, Clarendon Press, 1927).

[7] Renaissance hymns on the other hand have a vocabulary more derived from Classical poetry, and are therefore more artificial.

[8] There are, of course, two other hymns beginning in the same way, one by Claudianus Mamertus and the other by St Thomas Aquinas.

poet asks the cross to become soft and gentle to receive the limbs of the King of heaven:

> *Flecte ramos, arbor alta, tensa laxa viscera,*
> *Et rigor lentescat ille quem dedit nativitas;*
> *Et superni membra regis tende miti stipite.*[9]

This is in the old triumphal metre, the fifteen-syllable catalectic trochaic tetrameter. It was also that of the hymn for the dedication of a church, *Urbs Jerusalem beata* (modified by the seventeenth-century revisers to *Caelestis urbs Jerusalem*), which is of unknown date; these majestic verses evoke a splendid image of the new Jerusalem, the elect, as living stones polished by all their trials, part of that mystical building of which Christ is the corner-stone. Triumphal also is the poem of Theodulf of Orleans (ninth century), *Gloria, laus et honor*, of which the first six distichs have been kept in the liturgy as the hymn for the procession on Palm Sunday.

Some famous hymns have come down to us from the Carolingian renaissance, such as the *Sanctorum meritis* and the *Iste confessor*, both from unknown authors, and the *Ut queant laxis* of Paulus Diaconus. It was the first verse of this last that gave Guido d'Arezzo, at the beginning of the eleventh century, the names of the notes of the scale, which he took from the first syllables of the half-lines. The anthems of the Blessed Virgin, *Alma redemptoris mater* and *Salve regina*, also date from Carolingian times.

In the centuries that followed, rhythmic poetry based on accentual scansion, which was not completely new, as we have said with regard to the verse of Auspicius,[10] became normal for writers of sequences; at the same time rhyme appeared, heralding modern vernacular versification.

At first the sequence was simply the long-drawn out chant on

---

[9] "Bend your branches, great tree, slacken your taut fibres,
  Soften the hardness that nature gave you,
  And stretch the limbs of heaven's King gently on your stem."

[10] Commodianus had already confused the long and the accented syllable, and three hymns in rhythmic prose in honour of the Trinity are attributed to Marius Victorinus.

the final *a* of the alleluia of the Mass. Then fragments of text were substituted, to the same music, and the sequence became a separate poem, divided into verses like hymns and embellished with rhyme and assonance and a good deal of alliteration. There are more than five thousand of these sequences, the best period being the twelfth and thirteenth centuries. Many names ought to be mentioned, especially those of St Bernard and Adam of St Victor. The most famous sequences are still in the Missal; for example: *Veni, Sancte Spiritus*, attributed to Rhabanus Maurus (ninth century); *Victimae paschali laudes*, perhaps by Notker Balbulus (tenth century); *Lauda, Sion*, by St Thomas Aquinas; *Dies Irae*, of which the final version is by Thomas of Celano, a companion of St Francis; *Stabat mater*, by Jacopone da Todi (end of the thirteenth century), who was also using older material. For at that time the idea of literary property was somewhat vague, and no one was afraid to borrow this or that expression from older writers or the Bible. In the anthem *Salve, regina*, the words *filii Evae* are a set phrase found as early as St Augustine (*Confessions*, 1, 16, 25); *in hac lacrymarum valle* is taken from Ps. 83 and often quoted by the Fathers (e.g. Jerome, *Epist.*, 22, 10). The first words of the *Dies irae* are the beginning of a verse of the prophet Sophonias (1. 15): *dies irae, dies illa, dies tribulationis et angustiae.*

It must be stressed that in this abundance of sequences, as in the hymns—and we have room only to mention the finest—it is medieval Christendom which finds expression and which prays. Rhythmic poetry, as distinct from the products of the schools, appealed with its rhyme and alliteration to the ear of the people, and made things easier to understand and remember. The wide diffusion of these writings shows that they found a response in the minds of their hearers, just as today this humble Latin, revived and made alive again by the Gregorian chant, still helps, on great feasts when it is sung, to impose on our ears and on our hearts the solemnity of those occasions.

CHAPTER XV

THE CHIEF
CHARACTERISTICS
OF CHRISTIAN LATIN

The limits set to the size of this part of the book do not allow of
any treatment of the grammatical aspect of the Latin of Christian
authors.[1] Besides, if we leave aside a few Hebraisms and
Graecisms introduced by the translators, Christian writers con-
formed to the normal usage of post-classical times. It is in their
vocabulary rather that their originality is to be sought. Writers
like St Augustine were very much aware of this and he often
alludes to what we now call Church Latin: *ritus loquendi
ecclesiasticus* (*Enarr. in Ps.* 93, 3), or *ecclesiastica loquendi con-
suetudo* (*De Civ. Dei*, 10, 21), or again *usus loquendi ecclesiasticus* (*Nupt. et Conc.*, 2, 33, 55). So, in order to avoid calling the
days of the week by their pagan names Christians became
accustomed to call them *feria secunda*, *feria tertia*, etc.,
instead of *Lunae dies*, *Martis dies*; a usage preserved in the
liturgy. In the same way Sunday was called *dies dominica*, the
Lord's day, instead of *dies Solis*.

Clearly there was an ecclesiastical Latin: the liturgy, theology,
canon law, like all branches of human activity, had their own
special terminology. But we can go further and say that Christianity profoundly altered the appearance of classical Latin by
breathing into it a new life.

[1] On this subject the reader may consult my *Manuel du latin chrétien*
(Strasbourg, 1955), Part II. But it should be noticedt hat Christine Mohrmann
has insisted more in her books and articles on the grammatical originality
of Christian Latin writers.

More than the multiplication of compound or derivative words it is important to notice the development in the use of abstract words and the creation of new spiritual meanings. Sometimes these abstracts replace a personal pronoun: *obsecro te ignoscas tarditati meae*, "I beg you to excuse my slowness" (Jerome, *Epist*. 99, 2); in sermons, *vestra fraternitas* is equivalent to *fratres*, "brethren". Sometimes they are used in place of a concrete noun: *captivitatem reducere*, "to bring back the captives" (Vulg., Deut. 30. 3); or of an adjective: *voti libertate se obstringere*, "to bind oneself by a free oath" (Augustine, *Vid.*, 5, 6); or a verb: *stationem imperavit soli et lunae*, "he commanded the sun and the moon to stop" (Jerome, *Jov.*, 2, 15).

The creation of new spiritual meanings is, however, more important even than these habits of style. It is true that abstract words were made by Christians to translate ideas and concepts which were new and unable to be expressed in the more concrete classical language; but it is of greater importance to notice this other process, of taking a concrete word, or one referring to concrete things, and using it in a metaphorical or spiritual way. Thus, *compages*, "joint, connection", was used to signify the mystical union that joined the members of the Church in one spiritual body; the word *aedificatio* first has the metaphorical sense of building the Church, the kingdom of God, and then the building up of the faith in our own lives and those of others, and from this the spiritual meaning "confirming by good example, edification". Other examples will be given when we come to speak of the metaphorical and symbolic style.

RHETORICAL FIGURES

Without spending a long time on the figures of rhetoric properly so called, we must remark that the multiplication of allegorical symbols, of comparisons and metaphors, especially in writings intended for the mass of the people, were in Christian writers less a trick of style than the effect of a real desire to communicate truths and feelings which the writer wished to pour forth.

Two kinds of figures had a special value for Christians: antithesis and symbolism; for they had their origin in a new way of thinking. It was not new to oppose body and spirit: it was a common antithesis in ancient philosophy. But with the Christians it became a constant habit to oppose body and soul, flesh and spirit, spirit and matter, the life of this world and the life of the Christian, earth and heaven, what passes and what eternally remains: *qui occidunt corpus, animam vero non possunt occidere,* "those who kill the body, but have no means of killing the soul" (Matt. 10. 28). Such antitheses greatly helped to increase the solemnity of liturgical prayers, as we have already seen. Examples of other specifically Christian antitheses could be given, particularly those opposing faith and works, and the spirit and the letter.

As for the use of symbolism, for the Fathers of the Church it certainly was not a mere rhetorical device, and if it took on a new importance it was because it originally had an exegetical purpose: it was a question of showing, following the teaching of St Paul, that such and such a fact or character in the Old Testament prefigures what happened in the New. Besides, the parables of the Gospels were allegories that needed explaining, and even our Saviour's actions sometimes demanded a mystical interpretation. It was unfortunate that this became so artificial, so that symbolism was seen everywhere, and the smallest incident, the most ordinary character, even the lowliest animal was thought to express a symbolic meaning. But this is not directly relevant to the study of the Christian language; what is important is the influence symbolism had on the style and vocabulary of Christian writers.

Thus, we learn from Genesis that our first parents, after they sinned, were ashamed and covered their nakedness with girdles of fig-leaves; for St Augustine, this word "fig" evoked the idea of sin, and when Jesus says to Nathanael that he saw him "under the fig-tree" (John 1. 48), that means "in the darkness of sin" (*Serm.*, 89, 5 and 69, 4); the word has become a symbol. A writer could make play with this symbolism according to his fancy: so, for St Augustine again, these fig-leaves also symbolized

11—S.L.

uselessness: as opposed to the fruit, which are good works, the leaves are but vanity (*Trin.*, 12, 8, 13).

There is frequent mention of oil in the Bible: it is a sign of wealth (Prov. 21. 20); a food (Deut. 32. 13); it is used for the anointing of kings and priests, and for lighting (cf. the parable of the wise and foolish virgins) and also for the treatment of wounds. So in the Fathers the word "oil" became a symbol to be understood in a spiritual sense: it signified riches and fertility, but above all moral ideas, the charity of good works, gentleness, joy, justice: *absque oleo bonorum operum*, "without the oil of good works" (Jerome, *Epist.* 125, 19); *oleum miseri-cordiae*, "the oil of mercy" (Caes. Arelat., *Serm.*, Morin, p. 621); *unxit te Deus oleo exultationis*, "he has anointed thee with the oil of joy" (Ps. 44. 8 in Augustine, Enarr., 82, 2 = *oleo laetitiae*, Vulgate). Hyssop was understood as a symbol of purification (Lev. 16. 4; Ps. 50. 9). And such symbols from the Bible grew in numbers in the writings of the Fathers: Babylon meant the world, as opposed to the city of God; and everyone knows the names used of Christ: the Lamb, the Spouse.

METAPHORS

A growing need for a clearer and more striking expression of ideas that would awaken men's minds and touch their hearts led to a great increase in the number of similes and metaphors; for the Christian writer was not simply writing for the educated and intelligent, but for all men, even the most humble. To be understood by all, he had to rely on images drawn from the concrete world of nature all men had before their eyes, the sea, the flowers of the field, the products of the earth; or from the things every man could see in his daily work, in trades and crafts, in the army, in seafaring, in the courts, in commerce, in country life and even in the circuses and games. We have already remarked how martyrdom was compared to a struggle, and admiration for the winner was expressed in words like "glory", "triumph", "crown", "laurel", "palm" and "trophy". The number of martyrs was likened to a blossoming of flowers

—*quorum numerus effloruit* (Augustine, *Contra Faust.*, 22, 76); to a harvest bringing in a hundredfold (Cyprian, *Epist.*, 76, 6); to a cohort: *adest militum Christi cors candida* (Cyprian, *Laps.*, 2). The martyr is like a surveyor (*metator*) who goes ahead to mark our places in heaven (Cyprian, *Epist.*, 6, 4).

The metaphors for the blessedness of heaven are infinitely varied: the kingdom, dwelling-place of light, the eternal tabernacles, the palace, the house of the Father, our inheritance, our true homeland after the exile in this world; it is rest after a journey, a refreshment or consolation (*refrigerium*), a garden, a banquet, peace, final rest, the eternal sabbath, or octave, the Sunday eternally without evening: *pax sabbati, pax sine vespera* (Augustine, *Confessions*, 13, 35, 50). This is no matter of one man's happiness; it was a vision of a countless number from all the nations, a choir wherein the elect sang the glory of God. These elect also are likened to a harvest, or to the grain which is separated from the chaff by the Winnower on his threshing-floor at the Last Judgement.

Death was not an end; it was a crossing-over (*transitus*), a departure (*profectio*), a change of home (*migratio, commigratio*), a recall to God (*accitus, arcessitio, vocatio*), or again a sleep (*dormitio*) awaiting the resurrection.

Equally innumerable are the metaphors signifying the Church: a mother who bears children in the faith, who nourishes them on the milk of her teaching, whose womb has brought forth the martyrs and all the peoples of Christendom, by the breath of the Holy Spirit; she is the bride of Christ and the mystical body of which he is the head; she is a house, at whose door men come to knock to be changed and reconciled to God; a sheepfold over which the pastors must watch, and whose erring sheep have lost the way; she is sometimes compared to a camp in which the catechumens are the young recruits, or to an army, though this metaphor is mainly used for priests or religious.

A whole book would be needed to list the metaphors which have been used to signify the actions of God on his creatures, the love of Christ, the secret of man's conscience and the mystery of his soul, the ugliness of sin and the beauty of the Christian virtues, the base meanness of the flesh and the greatness of man redeemed; not to mention the many metaphorical expressions used for Christ, for the Blessed Virgin Mary, St John the Baptist, St John the Evangelist or St Paul. This astonishing profusion of metaphors, which some might judge decadent and which was certainly not in accordance with classical taste, was nevertheless due, not to a concern for rhetorical brilliance, but to an ardent desire to persuade, to convince, and to a growing need for better expression.

THE LANGUAGE OF CHRISTIAN FEELINGS

To characterize the renewal of the Latin vocabulary brought about by Christianity we must bring out the importance of the development of many new emotional shades of meaning, alongside of the creation of some neologisms needed to express the feeling and the idea of charity. In this the influence of the translations of the Bible was the determining factor, for the style of the Scriptures, with its power to stir the emotions, already possessed the essential elements of such an affective vocabulary as Christianity demanded. The Psalms especially, and the prophetical books, are informed with a passionate feeling of attachment to God, an ardent call to him, an inspired confidence in his protection and hope for the Messias; in the New Testament there is also charity, the love of men and attachment to Christ.

We have already noted the tendency of languages, in the later stages of their evolution, to multiply words compounded with prepositions. The preposition *ad* expresses a striving towards God in expressions like *totus ad Deum eram* (Jerome, *Tr. in Psal.* I, Morin, p. 157, 6), *ingemiscere ad Deum* (Salvian, *de Gubernatione*, 7, 11); it was the same in compound verbs, e.g. *accorporari in Christo* (Paulinus of Nola, *Epist.* 4, 1), "to come so close to Christ as to be one with him" (*incorporari* would not have expressed this idea of coming close); and in the following phrase we are far from the idea of simply passive rest: *quis mihi dabit acquiescere in te?* (Augustine, *Confessions*, 1, 5, 5), "Who will enable me to go to you and find rest?"

In many compounds the preposition *cum* signifies an approach of the Godhead towards us or a desire on our part to be united to the divinity, and particularly to share in the sufferings of Christ: *commortuus Domino suo* (Jerome, *Epist.*, 22, 39), an idea familiar to us also in St Paul's epistles; and the verb *compatior* carries the same suggestion. On the other hand *complaceo* signifies God's loving, his being well pleased with, his Son, or with man (Vulgate, Matt. 3. 17, etc.; 3 Kings 10. 9), or conversely man's contentment or confidence in the "faithfulness" of God: *complacui in veritate tua* (Ps. 25. 3). New terms were made by compounding with this preposition: *complacatio*, "contentment, indulgence"; *condelectatio*, "the act of delighting in (the law of God)"; *condescensio*, "condescension, lowering oneself (to our weakness)"; *conglorificari*, "to be glorified with (Christ)"; *consurgere*, "to rise (as Christ did)"; *consepeliri*, "to be buried (mystically with Christ)"; *convivificare*, "to make alive (in Christ)".

The enthusiasm for that which never ends, the need for the absolute, found expression in new compound adjectives, such as *indeficiens*, "unceasing, unfailing"; *indeflexibilis*, "unswerving"; *indesinens*, "unending"; *incommutabilis*, "unchangeable"; *immarcescibilis*, "incorruptible".

Purely affective also are such new words as *praeclarere*, "to reveal oneself in all one's splendour" (of Christ, in Sedulius and St Avitus); *praeconspicabilis*, "seen in all one's glory"; *superabundantia*, "superabundance (of grace)"; and, in the Song of the Three Children, *superlaudabilis et supergloriosus in saecula*, "praised above all, renowned above all, for ever" (Dan. 3. 53).

More numerous are older Latin words which gained a new emotional warmth. Thus *caritas*, which already in classical Latin meant "affection, love", was to express a mystical fervour by being used in a context more charged with emotion: *caritas Dei diffusa est in cordibus nostris per Spiritum Sanctum* (Rom. 5. 5); or by being used with a synonym: *affectu et caritate Christi* (Hilary, Matt. 30. 3). *Affectus* is similarly changed by the addition of an epithet: *intimo affectu* (Augustine, *Spir. et Lit.*, 26, 46), *pio affectu* (id., *Enarr. in Ps.* 86, 3).

The word *providentia* in Cicero, when speaking of the gods, signifies the purely intellectual idea of the divine foreknowledge; for Christians, an idea, a feeling, of loving care is added: *mira providentia et bonitas Creatoris* (Leo, *Serm.*, 6); *agnosce bonitatem Dei . . . ex providentiis . . .* (Tertullian, *Adv. Marc.*, 2, 4), "acknowledge the goodness of God in the kindly ordering of his providence". *Pietas* could mean for pagans piety, the respect of men for the gods; but could it signify any feeling of the gods for men? Virgil, expressing feelings which anticipate (if we may risk the word) in a mysterious way those of the Christian, wondered with a sort of anguish whether there was in the divinity a just regard for us: *si qua est caelo pietas quae talia curet* (*Aeneid*, 2, 536), "if there is in heaven any justice to take care of such things"; *si quid pietas antiqua labores respicit humanos* (*ibid.*, 5, 688), "if their ancient care has any regard for the labours of men". Christians, on the other hand, are sure of the goodness and mercy of God towards them, and it is precisely this that the word *pietas* means among them: *magna Dei propter salutem nostram benignitas pariter et pietas* (Cyprian, *Dom. Orat.*, 30); *ipsa bonitas et misericordia et pietas* (id., *Epist.*, 55, 23), "his goodness, his mercy and his loving-kindness". Much the same might be said about the words *benignitas, miseratio, misericordia, timor*, etc.

We can also notice this same transition from a purely intellectual meaning to an affective one in the semantic evolution of some verbs and certain nouns describing actions. So, the word *credere* does not signify simply a mental act but a feeling also, the feeling of trust and confidence: it is no longer a matter of a philosophical opinion but of a striving and a hope: *credo in Deum meum quod servum suum quem mihi promisit ostendet* (Jerome, *Vita Paul.*, 7); *in Christum credidimus ut det nobis vitam aeternam* (Augustine, *Enarr. in Ps.* 40, 3). And the construction of this verb with *in* and the accusative seems to express better than the simple dative this striving towards God or towards Christ. We have already noticed the different senses of *confiteor*. The verb *videre* is applied to mystical contemplation, just as in the Bible the prophets are called "seers" (Jerome,

Comm. Is., 1, 1, 1). *Contemplatio* is no longer only "reflection" as it was for Seneca, but a mystical state raising us above ourselves, either in this life: *penna contemplationis volare* (Gregory the Great, *Hom. Ezech.*, 3, 1); or in the next: *contemplationis eius ineffabilem dulcedinem* (Augustine, *Civ. Dei*, 7, 31).

This power to move the emotions as well as the mind is usually reinforced and made more specific by the context. Thus *Dominus* no longer signifies the severity of a Roman master if it is joined with epithets like *misericors, miserator, pius, dulcis, bonus*. In classical Latin, *misericordia* meant, it is true, "pity" or "mercy", but the word gains quite a new emotive warmth if, for example, God is called, in the Biblical manner, *fons omnium misericordiarum* (Augustine, *Enarr. in Ps.* 6, 10). Redundant synonyms contribute to the same effect, as when St Leo joins the words *pietas misericordiae* (*Serm.*, 55, 5) or *miseratio clementiae* (*ibid.*, 12, 2).

Lastly, figurative language was used to express in an emotive way the aspirations of the mystics, with such verbs as *amplector*, "to join oneself to"; *anhelo*, "to pant for, towards"; *clamo*, "to invoke or supplicate aloud"; *deficio*, "to falter, faint"; *esurio*, "to hunger after"; *inebrio*, "to be intoxicated"; *inviscero*, "to fix deep in one's heart".

We have not quoted examples from liturgical Latin, because that has been dealt with separately; but clearly such quotations would make it possible to draw an even more convincing picture. As we said at the beginning, we have restricted ourselves to the Latin of the patristic period. But if it did not overstep our present limits, we could dwell for a long time on the newness of the language of medieval piety.

Beside the austere and ancient formulas of the traditional liturgy, addressing God "through Jesus Christ our Lord", we find gradually arising a humbler prayer, that of a people "groaning and weeping", conscious of their own profound wretchedness and thinking themselves unworthy to speak directly to their Saviour, trying to soften his judgements by addressing themselves to his Mother, taking a loving pleasure in reminding him that he was once, like us, a child, and in repeating in an almost familiar way his sweet name of Jesus; a people, lastly, who had felt, perhaps in the persecutions, something of the infinitely pitiable sufferings of our Lord on the cross, with his Mother at his feet. Sometimes in the Middle Ages (and in our own days?) the times were very dark; but it is nonetheless true that the Middle Ages gave such expression to tenderness and gentleness as none other: that was their way of being Christian, in violent contrast to the harshness of men. Doubtless the later devotion to the Blessed Sacrament moved on a very much higher level; to appreciate these other more humble devotions properly we may have to rid ourselves of a certain philosophical and theological self-esteem. It is no novelty to say so, but it is important to stress it here, that all this flowering of religious literature and liturgy, the beginnings of which we saw in Venantius Fortunatus and which ends so greatly in the *Imitatio Jesu Christi*, all this was written, not in the already formed vernaculars but in Latin, in a Latin still living enough to voice their thoughts and feelings: this is what is so marvellous to us.

We could say very much the same things about the love of men and human charity; we could notice new compounds, like *coaegrotare* or *coinfirmari*, "to be sick with, to share the sufferings of"; *collaetari*, "to rejoice with"; etc.; or we could mark the new emotive power given to older words like *unio, unitas, unire*, beside such new compounds as *adunare, adunatio*; *affectus, amor, concordia, pax* and above all *caritas* and *dilectio*. In the homilies it was necessary to use the adjectives *carus, dilectus* in the superlative in order to express more fully the emotional meaning. *Beatus, beatissimus, benedictus*, expressed veneration in speaking of the dead, but they were also used when addressing the living: *consideremus itaque, benedicti* (Tertullian, *Praescr.*, 30).

Epistolary formulas became longer and more ceremonious than in classical times. These were not purely conventional clichés; they were inspired both by affection and respect: for example, *dilecte fili, carissime frater, desiderantissime, beatissime et venerande papa*. In the story of her pilgrimage Aetheria thus addresses her nuns in thought: *dominae venerabiles sorores*

(*Pereg.*, 2, 8); *dominae, lumen meum* (*ibid.*, 23, 10). Such feelings as we have just mentioned are well expressed in the conversational style by the vocatives *domina, domine* or *domne*: *domina soror* (*Pass. Perpet.*, 4), says Perpetua's brother when he visits her in prison; *curre, domne meus* (Vict. Vit., *Pers.*, 2, 30), says a grandmother encouraging her grandson. There is the same affectionate charity in St Augustine's *domne pauper* (*Serm.*, 14, 3, 4).

It goes without saying that this new affective sense is not spread uniformly throughout the writings of Christians; some controversial works, especially of Tertullian or St Jerome, are biting enough. There is no need to do violence to the facts, nor to try to reduce to a simple, single formula so many different writers of such various periods. There has been some argument, even heated argument, as to whether we should speak of "Christian Latin" or "the Latin of Christian writers". This battle of words should not affect us; it is enough to study the facts in all their complexity, without feeling obliged to sum them all up under one name, to put the same label on all. That would give the impression that the study was completed, whereas we should in fact have got no further forward.

According to some linguists to speak of "Christian Latin" is to take an anti-scientific stand in flourishing a name devoid of meaning. When I say "Christian Latin" am I really thought to have in my mind a single, clearly definable entity? Such a thing does not exist in the fluid state of linguistic science. It is simply a convenient, handy way of saying that I want to talk about Christian literature from a linguistic point of view.

But we cannot just leave it at that. Within Christian Latin there is room to distinguish first the vocabulary special to the Scriptures, and that of the liturgy, of theology, of scholasticism, of canon law; no one denies that what we may call "ecclesiastical" Latin has its own vocabulary. Then, it is legitimate and altogether natural to go further and consider Christian Latin as a whole. Whether we are dealing with the more specifically sacred language of the Scriptures and the liturgy, or with all Christian writers treating Christian subjects, we seem to be faced with a Latin very different from that of profane authors. And it is in the field more properly stylistic of mode of expression and emotive use of language that this difference is especially to be discovered.

Christianity put new life into Latin literature; that goes without saying. But it also put new life, a new warmth, into the language. And there are two aspects of this renovation, two aspects certainly not equally to be discerned in all writers, but still the most constant, from the first translations of the Bible and the *Passio Perpetuae* to the *Imitation of Christ*. These are the two aspects we have remarked on at the end of this study: an extraordinary development of the use of figurative language and of new, spiritual senses of words, and at the same time an increased warmth of emotional, affective language, to give expression to the love of God and the love of men.

SELECT BIBLIOGRAPHY

HEBREW

In this series: ALBERT GÉLIN, P.P.S.: *The Religion of Israel*; JEAN STEINMANN: *Biblical Criticism.*

ABRAHAMS, I.: *A Short History of Jewish Literature*, London, T. Fisher Unwin, 1906.

BEVAN, E. R., and SINGER, C.: *The Legacy of Israel*, Oxford and New York, Oxford Univ. Press, 1928.

DAVIDSON, A. B.: *An Introduction to Hebrew Grammar*, Edinburgh, T. and T. Clark, and New York, Scribner, 1932, 24th edition revised by J. E. McFadyen.

EPSTEIN, I.: *Judaism*, London and Baltimore, Penguin Books, 1959.

KOEHLER, L., and BAUMGARTNER, W.: *Lexicon in Veteris Testamenti Libros* (Hebrew and Aramaic/German and English), Leiden, Brill, 1953.

ROBINSON, T. H.: *The Genius of Hebrew Grammar*, Oxford and New York, Oxford Univ. Press, 1928.

STEVENSON, W. B.: *A Grammar of Palestinian Aramaic*, Oxford and New York, Oxford Univ. Press, 1924.

WAXMAN, A.: *A History of Jewish Literature*, four volumes, New York, Bloch, 1933–47.

WOOD, C. T., and LANCHESTER, H. C. O.: *A Hebrew Grammar*, 2nd edn, London, Kegan Paul, 1920.

GREEK

ARNDT, W. F., and GINGRICH, F. W.: *A Greek–English Lexicon of the New Testament and Other Early Christian Literature*, Chicago and London, Univ. of Chicago Press and Cambridge Univ. Press, 1957.

ATKINSON, B. F. C.: *The Greek Language*, 2nd edn, London, Faber, and New York, Macmillan, 1933.

CAMPBELL, J. M.: *The Greek Fathers* (Our Debt to Greece and Rome Series), London and New York, Longmans, 1929.

172 SELECT BIBLIOGRAPHY

MARROU, H. I.: *History of Education in Antiquity*, translated by G. Lamb, London and New York, Sheed and Ward, 1956.

MOULE, C. F. D.: *An Idiom Book of New Testament Greek*, Cambridge and New York, Cambridge Univ. Press, 1953.

MOULTON, J. H.: *Introduction to the Study of New Testament Greek*, 5th edn, New York, Macmillan, 1956; *Grammar of New Testament Greek*, Volume 1, *Prolegomena*, 3rd edn, Edinburgh, T. and T. Clark, 1908; Volume 2, with W. F. Howard, Edinburgh, T. and T. Clark, 1929; with George Milligan, *Vocabulary of the Greek Testament*, New York, Harper, 1930.

NUNN, H. P. V.: *The Elements of New Testament Greek*, 7th edn, Cambridge and New York, Cambridge Univ. Press, 1939; *A Short Syntax of New Testament Greek*, 5th edn, Cambridge and New York, Cambridge Univ. Press, 1943.

QUASTEN, J.: *Patrology*, two volumes, Westminster, Md, Newman Press, 1950 and 1953.

ROBERT, A., and TRICOT, A.: *Guide to the Bible: An Introduction to the Study of Holy Scripture*, two volumes, Westminster, Md, Newman Press, 1955.

ROBERTSON, A. T., and DAVIS, W. H.: *A New Short Grammar of the Greek Testament for Students familiar with the Elements of Greek*, New York, Harper, 1933.

SOUTER, A.: *A Pocket Lexicon to the Greek New Testament*, Oxford and New York, Oxford Univ. Press, 1916.

LATIN

CONNELLY, J.: *Hymns of the Roman Liturgy*, London, Longmans, and Westminster, Md, Newman Press, 1957.

HASKINS, C. H.: *The Renaissance of the Twelfth Century*, Cambridge, Mass, Harvard Univ. Press.

MOHRMANN, C.: *Liturgical Latin: Its Origins and Character*, London, Burns and Oates, 1959, and Washington, Catholic Univ. of America Press, 1957.

NUNN, H. P. V.: *An Introduction to the Study of Ecclesiastical Latin*, 3rd edn, Eton, Alden and Blackwell, and Naperville, Ill., Allenson, 1951.

PERKINS, M.: *Your Catholic Language*, London and New York, Sheed and Ward, 1942.

PLATER, W. E., and WHITE, H. J.: *A Grammar of the Vulgate*, Oxford and New York, Oxford Univ. Press, 1926.

RABY, F. J. E.: *History of Christian Latin Poetry from the Beginnings to the Close of the Middle Ages*, 2nd edn, Oxford and New York, Oxford Univ. Press, 1953.

RAND, E. K., *Founders of the Middle Ages*, Cambridge, Mass., Harvard Univ. Press, 1928.

SOUTER, A.: *Glossary of Later Latin to* 600 A.D., Oxford and New York, Oxford Univ. Press, 1949.

The Twentieth Century Encyclopedia of Catholicism

The number of each volume indicates its place in the over-all series and not the order of publication.

TWENTIETH CENTURY ENCYCLOPEDIA OF CATHOLICISM

All titles are subject to change.

Rev. Joseph M. Vignoe

CARMELITE MONASTERY
Beckley Hill
Barre, Vt., 05641

DATE BORROWED